Praise for *The Last Gifts*

Exquisitely written, *The Last Gifts: Creative Ways to Be with the Dying* is a heart-opening guide not just for health-care professionals but also for family members and friends of a person who is ill, disabled, or dying. From her disarmingly honest personal introduction to the compelling stories of the dying people themselves, Jillian Brasch gives us an emotional map of how to be genuinely helpful. You'll be able to use your own creativity to help the person you love through his or her illness with its physical, psychological, and spiritual challenges, right up to their death and your bereavement. Jillian Brasch and her patients model deep courage and unconditional love.

～ GAIL DONOHUE STOREY,
author of *The Lord's Motel* and *God's Country Club*

Jillian has written a compelling book, rich with insight and the satisfaction of small triumphs. The story of her experiences growing up reveals the quality of her spirit, and her creativity shines out of every description of her work. She draws her characters with such clarity and compassion that we feel we know each patient, in both shadow and sunshine. Jillian is a gifted writer, and she has given us stories and lessons that are simply told and thoroughly imbued with gentle wisdom. This book should be on everyone's reading list.

～ MARY STEPHENSON,
hospice volunteer director

These people stepped out of the pages and sat next to me as I read their stories. *The Last Gifts: Creative Ways to Be with the Dying* gave me a whole new level of understanding about how to live, not only among the dying, but also among the living. Now, I'm more present with my children and I listen to their *real* needs. After reading *The Last Gifts*, I have a desire to live more fully and not take life for granted. I was changed by it, made better by it, awakened by it, educated by it, and enlightened by it. This book shows us how to step beyond the obvious into the realm of *true* love.

⁓ LINDA LEIBOWITZ,
caregiver to her dying mother

My experience of my best friend's death would have been very different or possibly even traumatic without the wisdom and guidance in this book. Jillian's experience and insight were a profound gift to me—the gift of really being with my friend during the time of her death. Jillian helped me keep a loving, spiritual perspective through the transitions, which meant that I could be fully present with my friend in ways *she* needed. I will always be grateful.

⁓ PAIGE YOUNG CANNON,
caregiver to her dying friend

THE LAST GIFTS

"Grasping creates
suffering..."
Buddhist Philosophy

The
LAST
GIFTS

Creative Ways to Be with the Dying

JILLIAN BRASCH, OTR

Andrews McMeel Publishing, LLC
Kansas City

ISBN-13: 978-0-7407-7704-2
ISBN-10: 0-7407-7704-1

Library of Congress Cataloging-in-Publication Data

Brasch, Jillian.
  The last gifts : creative ways to be with the dying / Jillian Brasch.
    p. cm.
  ISBN-13: 978-0-7407-7704-2
  ISBN-10: 0-7407-7704-1
  1. Death--Social aspects. 2. Death--Psychological aspects. 3. Helping behavior. 4. Creative thinking. I. Title.

  HQ1073.B726 2008
  306.9--dc22

                              2008017991

08 09 10 11 12 MLT 10 9 8 7 6 5 4 3 2 1

www.andrewsmcmeel.com

ATTENTION: SCHOOLS AND BUSINESSES
Andrews McMeel books are available at quantity discounts with bulk purchase for educational, business, or sales promotional use. For information, please write to: Special Sales Department, Andrews McMeel Publishing, LLC, 1130 Walnut Street, Kansas City, Missouri 64106.

For Eddie

CONTENTS

I don't believe people are afraid of death.
What they are afraid of is the incompleteness
of their lives.

~ TED ROSENTHAL,
having been told he had leukemia at the age of thirty,
How Could I Not Be Among You?

Author's Note

In telling these stories as I experienced them, I have made every effort to protect the privacy of all individuals and institutions. All names are pseudonyms and some of the places and specific events have been fictionalized in order to protect privacy. I have tried to preserve the activities that we worked on together as accurately as possible.

I have intentionally tried to downplay the diagnosis when it was not relevant to the integrity of the story. They are all dying patients. I think it is more helpful to read about what each individual went through rather than read about their specific diagnosis.

Although I often refer to persons living their dying as "dying patients" and my time with them as "sessions," this is simply an efficient way for me to communicate in the format of this book. I specifically left out physical activities requiring medical training, with the exception of biofeedback. While this is only available to someone who has been trained to use it, there are other forms of relaxation and stress management that can also be used.

This book will be helpful to anyone in the proximity of a dying person. My intent is to share my experiences as an occupational therapist in order to encourage you to use whatever skills you've accumulated throughout your life to assist the dying, making their transition as rich and comfortable as possible.

ACKNOWLEDGMENTS

Knowing Cindy Pickard has enriched my life beyond measure. She invited me to work with the dying and said just the right words of encouragement when I was saying "Gee, I don't know. Sounds depressing." The open-hearted way she works with people is my continual inspiration.

Gail Donohue Storey gently pulled the stories out of me and then provided sensitive, thoughtful editing, infinite patience, generosity, and kindness. She is my guardian angel and I could not have written this without her.

Eddie Brasch gives me unfaltering love and support in all that I do. His enormous creativity and love of life heal me. I can't believe my luck.

I am eternally grateful to Allan Stark and Marc Winkelman who never lost faith in me or this book. I can also never thank Hugh Andrews enough for taking a chance, and Chris Shillig who held my hand and led me through the process of turning the manuscript into a book. I appreciate and respect her knowledge and editing.

Thanks to The Reverend Beth Sherman for the heartfelt bereavement ritual.

I want to thank Diane Breidenstein, Lori Burkhart, Piper King, Linda Leibowitz, Becky McGaughy, and Carol McKinney for early readings and support any time I needed it. I also want to thank Chuck Brasch, Randy Meek, and Amy Weidmann for their continued support.

Finally, I am grateful to the many patients I worked with at the end of their lives. Sharing your lives was a sacred privilege.

INTRODUCTION

"You do what? Work with people who are dying? Sounds depressing." I can't tell you how many times I've heard that, but if you keep reading you'll discover that it's not what you might think. By spending time with someone who is dying you are rewarded with intimacy that you might never have with anyone else. Mother Teresa said that she worked with the dying because they're closer to God. People who are dying usually get pretty clear about what's important to them. Talking with them puts me in touch with my own values. In a world where multitasking is the norm, they teach me the richness of being fully alive by focusing only on this moment. Because really, that's all there is.

It's not depressing—it's rich and clear and vibrant. That's not saying there aren't obstacles. That's what this book is about—dealing with those obstacles. I worked with people who were afraid, lonely, unmotivated, overwhelmed, confused, unable to move, and sometimes unable to speak. Does that sound uncomfortable? Well, initially it is a little. But if you just show up—wasn't it Woody Allen who said 80 percent of life was just showing up—and commit to listening, you will be rewarded with a richness you may otherwise never know.

I wrote this book because I believe that no one should go through the dying process alone. Yet every day, people are cut off from their communities, including families and friends, because there is nowhere in our society that teaches us how to be comfortable with a dying person.

The following stories, framed by my own personal experience, illuminate ways to engage rather than pull away. I don't want to pretend that it's never depressing. Sometimes it is. But overall, it's not depressing. *It's awe-inspiring.*

Every person sooner or later will know someone who is dying. My goal is to help you know how to be present and comfortable with that person.

It's easy to think of every excuse in the world not to spend time with someone who is dying because it's awkward and uncomfortable. I know because I've done it, too.

But if you choose to engage, the gifts of this intimate dance are three-fold. The caregiver gives her gifts of time and willingness to engage. The dying person in return gives the gifts of insight and intimacy. Each time I worked with someone who was dying, I learned immeasurably about myself. Unless you're given your own terminal prognosis, you will never feel more alive or closer to the truth than when you are with someone who is living their dying. And finally, the activity between the caregiver and patient often includes making symbolic gifts for other loved ones left behind, thereby providing some closure. If you provide end-of-life care in your own personal capacity, you turn what might have been regret into positive, lasting memories.

Every six months or so I try to imagine what it would be like if I were told I was going to die soon. This exercise helps me gain a little perspective, get in touch with priorities, and clean out a few closets—literally and figuratively. However, I can't really imagine what it would be like. The closest I ever got was a few years ago when my doctor called me at five o'clock on a Friday afternoon and reported in her overly cheerful voice that a spot had shown up on my latest mammogram and she wanted me to see a surgeon to get a biopsy. "Oh, it's probably nothing, but you need to get it checked." I hung up and began screaming and pacing. A woman from Sears was at my home measuring the windows for blinds in my foster son's room. I tried to catch my breath, tried to figure out what to do next. The woman tried to say something comforting but nothing worked. I knew she wanted to get out the door and away from me as soon as possible. I was scared and I felt alone. How could my doctor drop this news in my lap when I was with a complete stranger and it was too late to call the surgeon? I needed my entire support system nearby. I called my husband and then I began worrying about him because just three years before his mother had died of breast cancer. By the time he got home, a sense of unreality had moved into my body, much the same feeling as when you're first told someone close to you has died. First a sense of numbness swept through me, then a sense of calm, deeper than I had ever experienced. It was the weekend and there was nothing I could actively do to get more information until Monday. Time moved differently for me now. I didn't hurry. I deeply experienced every moment. Without actively willing anything, I found my priorities redefined.

But this was just one weekend. It wasn't the real thing. I hadn't been given a terminal diagnosis. The next week I saw a surgeon who assured me that everything was fine and the rich, deep sense of calm soon went away.

I don't know what a dying patient is really experiencing. I only try to listen to what they're saying and enable them to meet their final goals, whatever those may be.

I wrote this book to enable you as caregiver (family member, friend, partner, volunteer, or medical personnel) to be able to do the same. These are stories about the way people I worked with chose to live their lives after prognosis. I can't write concrete answers to specific problems because that's not the way it works. Just as the patient is creative and living in the moment, you and I must do the same. We cannot come to them with our ideas of how we think they should "complete" their lives. It's their life. It's their choice—their completion or incompletion.

Because they're the ones going through the experience of dying, they're the experts. They hold their own unique set of answers, not us. There is no need to be afraid of failing when trying to help someone. All we have to be able to do is listen and then we will know how to help them. You don't have to have special skills. You just have to be able to hear when they tell you what they want.

Dying is a very human state. The body will pass through many stages as it declines. This can be scary if you don't know what to expect. A doctor or nurse can answer questions based on a "typical" course for any particular diagnosis. It is somehow comforting to know what to expect physically.

My husband has a friend who is a rock climber. When they invited me to go climbing and I declined, his friend said, "Don't you want to get out of your everyday life and challenge yourself?" I had to laugh. In my work, I don't have an "everyday" life. I am challenged daily with thoughts, feelings, and fears that may totally distort my reality. I do things that scare me almost every day. I love the passion I experience when I'm not protecting myself. I love the intimacy. I love not being afraid to be human. It's almost like a meditation. I relax deeply, listen openly, and pay attention.

I invite you to share the rewards of intimacy through the stories that are the gifts of seventeen dying patients. These are stories about fearing, coping, loving, forgiving, and saying good-bye. My hope is that they will inspire and remind you to look within yourself to solve problems in your own creative way, drawing from your unique set of experiences. Trust yourself. You'll make mistakes and that's OK. That's part of the "human-ness" of it all. It's never too late to say, "Sorry, that wasn't very sensitive of me." If you guard yourself to the point of not relating, you can't help.

You don't have to be a family member or know someone's complete history to be with him now. He's on a journey. And you're just going to walk with him for a while. Carry his load. Help with the chores. Cook his meals. Provide lodging. Give him comfort in the simplest of ways. Whatever one does when helping someone along a path, a journey. Unburden him.

We all have the ability to be with someone during this process. You can face your fears by trying to put yourself in his place. Imagine being told that you have a terminal illness. You've lost your ability to perform work and many physical activities. You're hit with all the feelings to work through concerning your diagnosis. You feel useless and are afraid of what the future holds. You've lost motivation and the ability to set goals. Time often becomes an enemy rather than a friend. Now add to this other people's fears and expectations of how you should be handling yourself.

Hopefully, the following seventeen stories will help you acknowledge your fears, give you some tools to dispel them, and provide you with strength. The stories illustrate the naturalness of the whole process. They give guidance and permission to be creative and vulnerable. They show you how to let go of the process of what you're doing as the patient's values change. Each story exemplifies how the caregiver can learn to listen to the real needs of the patient.

In essence, working with the dying patient is about achieving a state of mind, one that is receptive and generous. It's not denying your judgments. It's reaching beyond them, living above them for a short while so you can be with your fellow human being. When you listen to his fears, desires, and needs, ask yourself what you can do to empower and support him. It's as clear and rich as a moment can be when you know you've done this.

I worked with a man named Joe who had lung cancer. He also had several strokes over the past ten years that left him with many perceptual problems. Just dressing and being at home alone were potentially dangerous activities. Joe was afraid to leave home. He looked drunk when he walked, but he hated carrying a cane because it made him feel even more off-balance. Consequently, he fell at times and usually ended up in the hospital, unable to remember how he had gotten there. His failing memory greatly increased his anxiety.

Joe didn't have the skills or maybe even the desire to be close to his daughters. But he made a point of knowing about the areas of their lives that fit into his value system—how much money they made, status, respect, position in the work community, and family life. He was too anxious to interact much with his young, active grandchildren, but he valued them from a safe distance.

Joe started most sessions by saying, "I'm so stupid. I never knew I'd be this stupid. I'm really messed up."

I started most sessions by saying, "Joe, you're not stupid. You could never have worked in a bank all those years if you were stupid. It's just the strokes that cause all these problems. You've been through a lot." I explained how strokes affected people. I got a calendar and wrote all of his activities on it to compensate for his memory problems. We talked about the jobs he'd held. We talked about his travels, where he'd lived, what kind of work he'd done. We talked about his wives, his children, his grandchildren, his accomplishments, and his regrets. We sat outside on pretty days because he needed some fresh air. He told me what he knew about his neighbors and their routines. We fed the cat if he hadn't been able to find the food on his own. I encouraged him to carry a cane and hold onto furniture when he was walking in the house. I sympathized that it wasn't easy, but neither were hospital visits. I got him a card to send his favorite nephew for his wedding because he was too insecure about his bladder control to attend. I brought his favorite cookies to the nursing home when he had to stay there for a few days while his daughter went out of town.

Although we were just sitting on the porch underneath the oak tree's shade, talking and waving at the neighbors, I believed that our time was filled with activity. We were discussing safety issues and stress management, recalling the past, stimulating memory, enriching his environment, increasing self-worth, decreasing isolation, having him carry on in his role of parent/advisor.

Joe and I created many special moments sitting under that tree talking about old cars (he had been a car salesman for a while), reprimanding people who didn't stop for the stop sign (they were a safe block away), and just enjoying each other's company. He advised me to be careful as I drove away and I assured him that I would be here next week. As I drove away, he tilted his head and slowly lifted his hand to wave good-bye, almost a soft salute. This was his posture every week during our parting and it was his posture the last time we were together. I saw him as he wanted the world to see him—a man with many life experiences, well traveled, intelligent, dignified.

Although I have tried to point out process and outcome through Joe, it is important to recognize that some activities involve only process while others involve outcome. Sometimes I just wash my horse, not because he's exceptionally dirty or because we're going somewhere, but just because I want to wash him. My husband usually points out that my horse will probably roll in the dirt as soon as I'm finished. That's all right with me. It's just the process. He seems to like the cool water, back rub, and attention. I'm not asking anything from him. I'm not riding him or exercising him. No demands. Just a process. Just a way to be with him that's nurturing.

I remember meeting Paul's anxious wife at the door on my first visit to their home. She told me that her husband was bored and restless. She was convinced that what would really help him would be to build a ship in a bottle. She was adamant about this and told me several times that this is what I needed to help him do. Now that's a pretty unrealistic task for someone a couple of months away from dying. Yes, he was restless, but his energy was better channeled into working in his rose garden than performing a tedious task. He began cutting the fresh roses and giving them to his visitors. He got calmer as he gave these gifts to his friends and hospice workers. It gave him a daily focus other than himself. It's so important to feel that you have something to give back.

Paul also made a video with Cindy, another therapist who worked with him, and her son. It was totally unstructured. His dog and parrot were in it. He walked into view and away from the camera as he went about his activities, more like a home movie you make of your children doing whatever they're doing, rather than "performing for the camera."

I've seen family member after family member try to get the patient to do a specific activity. Some are good ideas while others are not. Often, the patient refuses until someone outside the family makes the same suggestion. I think this must be extremely frustrating for family members. And I think there could be a lot of reasons why this happens. Maybe it's too emotionally challenging to engage in the activity with a family member. Maybe the family member is pushing a little too hard and the patient needs the control of saying no. Maybe they need the project broken down into manageable tasks so it isn't so overwhelming. Sometimes I just think it takes the impetus of new energy to take a risk. ❧

I didn't need books. I didn't need crossword puzzles. I didn't need company. I could just sit there and enjoy my environment. Look out the window. I could see the birds for the first time in my life. Instead of just looking at the birds and just saying, "Ah yes, birds," I could see them, without calling them birds; without seeing them as being something. I could see the sky. I could see the clouds and I could lay back and people could talk around me and I could be so receptive to what anybody was saying and yet at the same time just be watching the birds fly across the sky. That's all I could feel, that's all I could care about, without even caring. Just feeling that they were flying through the empty cage of my mind. It was just an open, full, rich feeling.

~ TED ROSENTHAL,
How Could I Not Be Among You?

THE
LAST GIFTS

My Story

In the fifties, my parents were considered old for having a baby. I was obviously not a planned child but a surprise. They had their children, now seven and nine years old, and it was quite a blow to them to have a new baby. I remember going on vacations when I was around four or five and hearing people comment on their granddaughter—meaning me. As a teenager, I regretted not having younger, more attractive parents. As a young adult looking back, I learned to appreciate the foresight, patience, and wisdom that only older parents could have given me.

By today's standards, they weren't all that old. Mother was forty; Dad was forty-six. But nutrition and exercise weren't the priorities they are now. Mother wouldn't get on the floor with me because she was afraid she couldn't get back up. My parents weren't healthy by anyone's standards.

Dad had broken his right leg while playing football when he was nine. The treatment at that time was to freeze the knee. So all of my life he had a stiff right leg. He walked oddly, swinging his right leg through the gait. He braked with his left foot when driving. When we went out, we always needed to be careful of where Dad sat so his leg would have enough room (no booths at restaurants, right-end stadium seating only).

It seemed that Dad had tremors all of my life. He was a nervous man, so I thought that was the cause of the tremors. As I understood it, that's what nervous people did—shook. When I was in high school, he was diagnosed with Parkinson's disease. As a young man, he had gotten encephalitis during an epidemic, soon after he and mother had met. Many people didn't survive, and a group of those who did later developed Parkinson's, like Dad. I learned about this years later in college when studying the epidemic.

Dad also had heart disease all my life. At a young age, I was taught to bring him his "heart pills" and to place a pill underneath his tongue if he was unable. I also remember him placing his hands on his chest in Fred Sanford style and "threatening" to have a heart attack if I was doing something he didn't like. It became a way to control my behavior. "Don't cry. You'll give Dad a heart attack."

When I was in the fifth grade, my parents were involved in a serious car wreck. Mother survived the wreck without too much physical trauma but Dad broke his right leg and got a head injury. His life, and consequently our lives, were never the same.

My grandmother (Dad's mother) came to stay with us for a few weeks after the wreck, but she didn't have much patience with children. Because both my parents had always worked long hours at our family-owned grocery store, we didn't have structured family activities. We ate meals individually, so I tended to read comics or watch TV when eating. We all ate different foods, depending on our likes and dislikes. Rather than an everyday occurrence, it was a big event when Mother was able to cook a meal. I spent many long hours at the grocery store. My sister tells me as a baby I was placed in a shopping cart while Mother worked.

After the wreck, Dad became obsessed with dying. He had always expressed a fear of death after dealing with his leg surgeries, encephalitis, and heart disease but now it became an obsession. (His way of dealing with my maternal grandparents' deaths was to get drunk.) The only time I saw Dad's best friend visit him at our house (instead of the store) was during this time. I remember Dad organizing his funeral plans and other instructions for Jim to carry out if he died. I remember he cried briefly, and was almost hysterical for a few moments as he talked to Jim. I didn't know men cried.

After the wreck, Mother ran the store. Dad eventually was able to go in for a few hours in the middle of the day, but it made him extremely nervous. So we all worked even more at the store to help Mother.

Something else important happened that year. Our president was assassinated. I was two years out of the third grade, where I had feverishly worked on my American Heritage folder. I had picture after picture of the first family glued in it. I fantasized for hours about them. I tried to imagine what it would be like to be Caroline Kennedy. What was it like to have young, healthy, good-looking parents? How did she feel now? I had had some close calls of almost losing my dad, but hers had actually died. How could they possibly survive? I had never known anyone without a dad and it was inconceivable to me. There was certainly no one to talk with rationally about all of these feelings, fears, and fantasies.

During the next six years, my dad became less and less able to cope with everyday life (from the head injury, from which he never fully recovered, and from alcoholism). As his physical and mental capacity diminished, death was always on his mind. He was terrified of dying and convinced it was lurking just around the corner.

Around Easter during my junior year in high school, Dad had a stroke. He had been taking a nap and when he awoke, he couldn't talk or get out of bed. I didn't know what to do so I called Mother at the store and told her I thought she should call an ambulance, since I was unable to make the decision myself. I remember feeling afraid and alone. When they took my dad out on the stretcher, they placed the sheet over his face to block the bright spring sun. Of course, they place a sheet over someone's face when they die, and that was all I could think about. I was sure, this time, he would die.

But he didn't. Once again, our lives were changed forever. He came home from the hospital at about the same time that school was out for the summer. I became his primary caregiver, so this was the first summer of my life that I spent more time at home than at the store. Once again his mother showed up to help out. Except now she was older, blinder, and even less tolerant of me as a teenager than as a child. Basically, I ended up taking care of both of them. I soon resented the added burden of cooking a separate meal for her special needs, reading the newspaper to her, and listening to her criticisms. The one advantage of having her there was that she took care of Dad while I went out with my boyfriend for a few hours every Friday night. He lived on a farm, which meant he also worked all week. A phone call was long distance then so we were never able to talk on the phone, but he always showed up on Friday night.

Back home it would be another week of taking care of Dad and Mommom. I talked with girlfriends on the phone but it was a summer of isolation for me. Dad was confused now. Every day he walked to the end of the driveway in his pajamas and tried to start his car. Mother had hidden the keys. Dad said he just needed to go home. We'd moved some of my grandparents' furniture into our home after their deaths and I guess it didn't look like our home to him. I remember getting so frustrated one day that I sat down on my bed and cried. Instead of threatening to have a heart attack, he came in and petted me on the head, and said, "It's OK, little girl." He didn't know my name. I looked into his eyes and knew that he knew me; he just didn't know my name.

As it got closer to the time for school to start, my oldest sister, Jane, who was in medical school at the time, came home to help Mother make the inevitable decision about what to do with Dad. My other sister, Judy, was married with children of her own and living in Florida. It was a small town and there weren't many resources. The only option was to put him into the nursing home.

In the beginning, I visited him, but as he became more and more disoriented, I visited less. Often, I took a friend with me for support because I was afraid to go alone. It was awkward and I never knew what to say or do. Dad was never able to call me by my name. I didn't understand anything about strokes. I made up excuses to tell my friends: "Oh, when someone's in bed a lot, their mind wanders and they can't remember things."

I felt terrible guilt that because I had to go back to school Dad had to go live in a nursing home. I felt despair, anger, and confusion. I started spending time with the school counselor since this was my senior year and I needed to pick a college. All my life my parents had encouraged independence, knowing that they were older and probably wouldn't live through much of my adulthood. I remember going to the bank with Dad when I was four and five to make deposits into my savings account for college. I had a checking account before any of my friends. I learned to drive on our farm when I was twelve and had a 1950 Plymouth waiting for me when I got my license at fourteen. I was able to drive to the nearest large city before any of my friends. I worked in our store. I was encouraged to make my own decisions; and after Dad got sick, Mother wouldn't make any decisions about the store without asking my opinion. Of course, all of this independence came with responsibility and I was still a kid. I needed to escape. There was never any talk of not going to college. The only question was "which one?" This gave me a reason to visit the counselor. She provided me with college catalogs, which I studied endlessly, trying to make a decision. Eventually, I started talking. She supported me by listening—unconditionally and confidentially. By being supportive without directing me, she allowed me to make a decision about college. I think the main concern was not academics, but distance. I needed to be far enough away to be separate from my family, yet close enough to be home within a few hours in case of an emergency.

By now, my college fund had been spent on medical bills. Someone suggested joining the service as a financial route to college; but with my parents in poor health, I couldn't make that kind of commitment. I thought of nursing school, but at the time my biggest fear was that I might check on a patient and find him dead.

I began college the same week I graduated from high school, just to get away from my family responsibilities. If I was four hours away, I didn't have to go by the nursing home to see Dad, or worse, feel guilty for not going by. I didn't have to see Mother's pain and stress and help her make business decisions on a daily basis. And, after all, I was fulfilling a goal of theirs by going to college.

Dad died the second semester of my freshman year. There were no good-byes, no finished business, no symbolic gestures. I had no good tools to deal with his illness and death, although much of my life revolved around this. And now he was gone.

Mother had a stroke my third year of college. Although we had studied strokes (and now I understood Dad's behavior better), I initially couldn't comprehend Mother's limitations. When I got to the hospital, she was in physical therapy. Here was the strength of my family, with a paralyzed right side and a catheter bag full of urine attached to her wheelchair. When the physical therapist showed me the slight movement Mother had in her right arm, I couldn't believe it. This was my mother, after all. I almost scolded her, "Mom, move your arm."

Mother was never able to work at the grocery store after her stroke. She had a caregiver stay with her for a while, but the woman was older and unable to perform some of the heavier tasks. I knew that one of the sweetest things for Mother was when I came home to visit, because I could safely get her in and out of the bathtub. She only had sponge baths when I wasn't there. I would massage her neck and shoulders afterward. It was heaven for both of us. Unlike my experience of being with Dad, I had activities I could do with Mother.

Mother was given a prognosis of two years. After she lived two years she began smoking again, knowing it was suicide but enjoying herself more with this simple pleasure she had known most of her life.

Later that year, Jane and Mother visited me. Jane turned to Mother and said, "Aren't you happy? You can be proud of all your children. Judy's married to a wonderful man and they have three great children. I'm out of medical school and working at a job I love in California. And Jill's got a job as an occupational therapist and has this wonderful little house. You've done a good job. You don't have to worry about us anymore." It struck me that Jane had released Mother of her "responsibility" because her life now seemed to revolve around worrying about her daughters. A week later she had a massive stroke while visiting Judy in Dallas. She had seen us all one last time. She had the stroke with the daughter who could best take care of her. When she woke up during my visit with her in the intensive care unit, she couldn't speak but held up her left hand, indicating her ring finger with her thumb. I knew exactly what she was trying to communicate because she had discussed her fear with me after her first stroke. I assured her that we had her wedding ring; it hadn't been stolen. She relaxed, shut her eyes, and went back into a deep sleep. I wanted to crawl up in bed with her and feel her peaceful breathing, but didn't. I got as close to her as I could and I released her, too. I told her that I knew it had been hard for her to live with the first stroke and that if she needed to go now, we would all be OK. I told her that I loved her and that I was glad she was my mother. She went into a coma and never opened her eyes again. She was diagnosed as brain dead a few days later but continued to live three more weeks. Judy visited her faithfully, as often as permitted. She kept insisting that Mother would get better but Jane and I knew the inevitable and talked by phone daily, trying to digest it all. With all the symbolic gestures and medical knowledge of what was going to happen, it was still a shock when Jane called to tell me the news.

I was working in a psychiatric hospital at the time and when I returned to work a week later, a nurse I didn't know very well pulled me aside. She confided that her mother had died and a year later she woke up one morning and couldn't go to work. She offered an ear if I needed anyone to listen. I thanked her politely but judged her as being pretty unstable. A year later I woke up with a sorrow so great that I couldn't go to work. I was only beginning to understand the grieving process.

Save Me from the Occupational Therapist

Preserve me from the
occupational therapist, God. She means well,
but I'm too busy to make baskets.
I want to relive a day in July when Sam and I
went berrying. I was eighteen; my hair was long
and thick, and I braided it and wound it round
my head so it wouldn't get caught on the briars.
But when we sat in the shade to rest,
I unpinned it, and it came tumbling down.
And Sam proposed.
I suppose it wasn't fair to use my hair to make
him fall in love with me, but it turned out to be
a good marriage. . . . Oh, here she comes, the
therapist, with scissors and paste.
"Would you like to decoupage?"
"No," I say, "I haven't got the time."
"Nonsense," she says, "you're going
to live a long, long time."
That's not what I mean; I mean that all my life
I've been doing things for people, with people.

I have to catch up on my thinking and feeling.
About Sam's death, for one thing. Close to the
end, I asked if there was anything I could do. . . .
He said, "Yes, unpin your hair." I said,
"Oh, Sam, it's so thin now and gray."
"Please," he said, "unpin it anyway."
I did and he reached out his hand—
the skin so transparent I could see the blue
veins—and stroked my hair. If I close my eyes,
I can feel it. Sam. . . .
"Please open your eyes," the therapist says.
"You don't want to sleep the day away."
She wants to know what I used to do. Knit?
Crochet? Yes, I did those things and cooked
and cleaned and raised five children and
had things happen to me. Beautiful things,
terrible things. I need to think about them,
arrange them on the shelves of my mind.
The therapist is showing me glittery beads.
She asks if I might like to make jewelry. She's a
dear child and means well so I tell her I might.
Some other day.

⁓ ELISE MACLAY,
Green Winter: Celebration of Later Life

I was this kind of occupational therapist. As a new graduate, I felt that I
needed to prove myself, and I went to work as supervisor of the occupational therapy department at a large psychiatric hospital. I inquired
about a patient's interests and background. Then I started them on a

leisure project with familiar qualities so I could evaluate their abilities to advance to more complex tasks. Or I taught them basic living skills that everyone needs to know—home management, balancing a checkbook, planning and cooking a meal. It was my job to see that they had life skills when they left the hospital. So while many of them could have taught me about how they had adapted this far in life outside the hospital, I taught them instead. I was, after all, the therapist. All of the patients were seen in groups so it was difficult to personalize therapy. The adults I worked with were older than me. Goals often had to be generalized for a wide range of people, not specific to the individual's needs. I worked hard to make the groups stimulating, entertaining, fun, and productive. But I left the hospital every day feeling that my therapy had not been personalized enough to be of real value. The patients most likely to slip through the cracks did not make much progress in therapy, and I didn't have time to really listen to them and their needs.

No one seemed to have much time. Medicine was just on the verge of becoming big business. I rushed from meeting to meeting, and worried incessantly about motivating the therapists in my department to do good jobs when we were all stretched too thin to be of much benefit. I tried to be happy with the "I did the best I could" frame of mind but I always felt too hurried—too busy being with all the patients to be with *any* of the patients. Somewhere in this rush I learned to treat the diagnosis rather than the person. I didn't respect the way I was treating patients. I became outwardly cynical with my colleagues, and I began to dread going to work. I was young; I had a great position early in my career but after three years, I quit and said that I never wanted to work in health care again.

After a couple of years, a friend asked me to do some part-time work in a rehabilitation center. Since I'd be able to work with patients individually, I decided to give it a try. I saw patients in thirty-minute time slots. Even if someone was sick, it was my job to make sure they worked the full thirty minutes so I could charge them. And after all, they couldn't stay on a rehabilitation unit unless they did rehabilitation. In contrast, if someone was feeling good and we were really making progress and could have worked for two hours, too bad, they were on a schedule and they needed to go to another type of therapy. Some of the patients I saw were embarrassed by the childish tasks I asked them to perform, like stacking blocks or tossing a balloon to strengthen their weakened arms. While some of this is developmental and therefore helpful, we also needed to work on how they would cope with their individual disabilities when they returned home. They often made progress in therapy, but fell apart after they got home. So, once again, I became disillusioned with health care and said I'd never do it again.

Time passed and a friend asked me to do some hospice work. There was little written about occupational therapy in hospice work so we had few guidelines. When we got our first patient, we spent hours talking about what to do, how to do it, how to write it up for the medical chart. Soon, it became the most natural thing in the world. There were no dictates of time here—work with the patient for twenty minutes or two hours, whatever they were able. Let the patient tell you what they need to do. Figure out a way to help them do it. I was often in the patient's home, taking cues from their surroundings, involving their family if there was one, and encouraging the patient to lead the way. It didn't matter whether a patient's problems were emotional or physical, I got to work with the *person* and deal with the problems they were facing today. We might work on memory and reminiscing in one session, then how to conserve energy while preparing his own meals at the next. Perhaps we'd work on managing stress or make gifts for saying good-bye to loved ones. I got to use all the skills I'd been taught and had more personal, unhurried sessions with my patients. Cynicism went out the door. Love walked in.

Some Basic Tools

Listening

Listen softly. A bird is singing. A dog is barking; farther away a dog barks in response. Listen gently, with your entire body. Listen with your individual cells. Listen for what your fellow human being needs to say. Listen for what you need to hear and at the same time, surrender all your needs. Listen with your heart.

Viso taught me a lot about listening. Viso was a horse from Peru whose name was a Spanish word meaning "brilliance." My husband, Eddie, and I first saw Viso in a recently plowed field. He was kicking up a storm of dust behind him; his conformation was beautiful; and his movement was effortless. He was elegant and he looked like an athletic powerhouse. Viso seemed to be everything my husband was looking for in a horse and he had to have him. The owner said the horse was dangerous and refused to sell him, and nothing Eddie said could persuade him otherwise. A couple of months later the owner called and told my husband that he had been working with Viso and now felt he was safe. However, before we loaded Viso into the trailer to take him home, the owner pulled Eddie aside to give him a chance to back out of the deal. "This horse has been severely abused," he said. "See these deep scars on his tongue?"

During our visit with Viso, my husband had ridden and played with him without any serious problems. He felt he could provide the TLC to heal Viso—so we took him home. That first night we petted and talked to him, trying to make him feel comfortable in his new paddock. The next morning we let him out to explore his small pasture, but couldn't catch him again without chasing him into a stall. He shook uncontrollably as we tried to get a halter on him. Every muscle in his body tensed as he snorted and danced nervously. I decided to just practice being with him, however he was. I went into his pasture and just relaxed. I let all the tension out of my body and mind and practiced being soft and receptive. Then I practiced patience. I gave him my attention and listened to his every move, without intent. Gradually, I talked to him and when he relaxed, I praised him. Nothing more. No expectations. It was a dance between the two of us. I had to listen carefully enough to his body (posture, facial gestures, eyes, and breathing) to know when I could step closer to him—when I could encourage him yet let him know he was in a safe place. This was a slow process but finally he could be touched without trembling and the fear in his eyes disappeared.

Viso taught me that I need to listen the same way to my patients. They're hurting in some way—physically, emotionally, or spiritually. I should be soft and receptive and listen with my whole being and not push, but when I hear a sign of acceptance, I need to encourage. It may be as simple as a sigh.

Patients will tell you what they need if you are able to listen.

Listen in the present moment.

We're so accustomed to doing many things at once in the midst of a lot of stimuli that it's often difficult to slow down our thoughts enough to just listen. Often, the most difficult part about listening for me is staying in the present moment. What another person says may stimulate memories, emotions, and questions, and my mind is off on a whole new track while he continues to talk. Since I'm listening and don't want to interrupt, I may write down a key word so I can mention it later. It seems like such a simple thing that it's almost not worth mentioning, but it frees me up to continue listening without trying to remember what I want to ask him next.

When I'm with a patient, I try to experience each moment as if it is the most precious in my life, because in hospice work, I never know when it just might be.

When I worked in a rehabilitation hospital, occupational therapy was done in one large room so there were usually about a dozen people working at the same time. I wanted to be like Joanna who was outgoing, motivating, and fun. You could hear what she and her patient were doing anywhere in the room. I am a fairly quiet person and saw this as a handicap. My supervisor reframed it for me when I got my evaluation. She said that when she looked out into the clinic from her office, it seemed there was an invisible room around my patient and me. She said that she didn't know how I did it, but in the middle of a busy room I created a private space that had only two people in it. I was just listening.

Don't compete, just listen.

I used to know a man who always responded to a story of mine with a similar, but somehow bigger story. If I said I was in a car wreck, I heard about a terrible car wreck he'd been in years ago, much worse than mine. I was asking him to listen to my feelings—not compete with his own stories.

When I'm listening to a person and I have a memory about a similar situation, I am tempted to share or compare my story. There's a fine line of whether I'm going to be perceived as sharing or competing. I ask myself whether my story will bring us closer together or further apart. Will it show that I understand what he's saying or simply be a distraction?

It seems the more intimate the story and the more vulnerable the person, the more intrusive it is to respond with a story of my own. I know when I have a crisis in my life that I need to talk about, I don't want to also be burdened with the story of someone else's crisis. I just need to be heard.

Be where the person is in their life and faith.

I occasionally work with people who view their dying process as punishment for not leading a better life. I also work with people who die angry or in denial. Though I may ask questions to help a patient explore his feelings, I feel I have no right to say how anyone should die. I can only offer my feelings about the person, not his beliefs. I can offer love and spaciousness to let him go through what he needs to experience.

This is much more difficult when the dying person is a family member or close friend. I may feel that, because I know the person so well, I surely know what's best for him. But again, my highest gift is to offer love and spaciousness.

Silence is inviting.

If I'm having a conversation, the exchange flows back and forth. But if I've committed to listening, I need to become comfortable with silences. Silences create time and space for feelings to be processed. Silence is an invitation for more. *I'm continuing to be here with you while you're saying whatever you need to say. And I'm not going to interrupt with my thoughts or judgments no matter how much I'm convinced I could fix things if I could just convince you to change your mind, think like me, etc. I'm not going to interrupt at all unless I see that you need encouragement to continue.*

Take responsibility for your feelings, but not theirs.

Clyde, a patient with a bird dog in his backyard, often told stories about other dogs he'd had or hunting trips he'd taken. He told me about a dog who wouldn't obey him, so he whipped it with a chain. He took it on a hunting trip, and when he stopped at a gas station he beat the dog again. "Turned out to be one of the best damn dogs I ever had," he said.

I love dogs. I felt sick at my stomach when he told me this story. I wanted to go home.

Listening without judgment is impossible. If I deny my judgments, then I'm protecting myself and creating distance. But if I accept my judgments and recognize them for what they are, I can create a spacious place in my mind to work above them in this moment. I can always deal with my feelings later. But right now, I'm going to be in this moment and hear his pain.

Don't assume, ask questions.

You can often learn a lot about someone through his environment. If he's in his own home, there will probably be pictures or paintings to give you clues about who this person is. Ask questions about the pictures. Ask questions about other family members. Learn who is important to him. Listen. Don't assume anything about relationships. Many people spend their lives with people they resent. It is a gift and a great relief to be able to feel safe enough to admit intimate feelings: fears, failures, and dreams. What does his home look like? Is it formal or casual? Cozy or stark? Are there handmade objects? Did he make them? Is it messy or organized? Was it organized before he got sick and messy now? Are there trophies, pets, plants, cookbooks? Is the pet a joy or is it now a burden? Ask questions. Is that chess set a hobby or merely a decoration? Is the home a reflection of his own personal style or did someone else decorate?

If the patient is in a nursing home, sometimes he can bring his own furniture. Why did he choose those pieces to bring with him? Are there familiar pictures? It may be a stark room and he may like it that way. What's stark to one person may be calming to another. Are there items that can be brought to make the room more personal, cozy, and just a nice place to be? Can the environment be enriched with colors, greeting cards, personal memorabilia? Can it be decorated for holidays?

What kind of work did he do before he got sick? Is he still working or is he retired? If a patient tells me he was a farmer, I can't assume this was a choice. It may have been his life's dream or he may have simply inherited a farm. He may have needed to support a family and farming was what he knew. If he'd had a choice, what would he have rather done?

What's his role in the family—son, brother, father, grandfather, provider? What is most important to him to continue?

What did he do for fun? Can he still do any of his previous hobbies? What does he do for fun now? Are there hobbies he's always wanted to try but didn't? Does he read, watch TV, visit with friends, e-mail, or talk on the phone?

Of course, if you're a family member or close friend your questions will be quite different from these. Just try to follow the same guidelines. Try not to assume that you know what he's feeling, no matter how well you know him. Let him lead the way in saying what's important for him today, knowing that it may change tomorrow. Know that he may tell each person in the family a different story as his ability to relate to each person develops and changes. It's much more difficult to listen to a friend or family member talk directly about his upcoming death, but you are giving each other the most intimate gifts you have by doing this.

Listen for the first sign of fatigue. Know when to quit for the day.

Keep it simple

Although there are complexities of relationships and feelings that I may never understand, I only try to deal with what is happening at this very moment as I am sitting beside the patient. What is he saying that he needs, and how can I help him accomplish it? All I need to do is travel with him this minute, hour, or day. He may be asking me to prepare something for the future and I am making a note of that. But I am living this moment as if there won't be a next visit. I've learned too often that there's not. What can I do right now to make his journey lighter? If he dies today, did I invite him to tell me what he wanted to do with the rest of his life? Did he tell me that he wanted to make a video for his children, so that even if it doesn't happen, they still receive the gift of knowing that he wanted to do this for them?

How to use this book

This is not a recipe book for doing activities with dying patients. There are no concrete answers within these pages. Just as if you were working with a dying patient, friend, or family member, I want to ask you to take a few minutes to deeply relax before you read. Readers will interpret the stories differently, depending on their life experiences and perceptions. Become intimate with this book. When something from a story sparks an idea for you, jot it down in the margin. For example, if I'm writing about relaxation, you may think of a technique of your own that you want to introduce to someone you're working with. Or you might remember techniques that you've tried in the past that have worked for you. Feel free to mark in this book. Draw pictures. Write names. Underline. Play. Turn it into a usable book—not one that you read and set on the shelf, never to use again.

Open your heart to the people in these pages. What do you hear them saying?

This book is an invitation to intimacy. I hope it provides some guidance and comfort while acknowledging and dispelling some fears. I hope that the stories serve to enlighten that there is no one certain way to die. My goal is to help you access your own personal strength and share it with another.

You don't need to remember names or know medical terminology or disease processes. Just sit back and go on this journey with me. We'll go into an assortment of living situations (homes, nursing homes, comfortable, poor, orderly, chaotic, solitary, surrounded by family); meet a variety of people (young, old, men, women, gay, married, single); and look at their illnesses, coping styles, and needs. I want to show that dying is as natural as any other process in our lives. And I want to share not only the pain, but also the great joy in this intimate dance.

The Hospice Angels

Mr. Dogan

Mr. Dogan and his wife had tried a nursing home for a couple of months but didn't much care for it. Now they were back at home—a new home—but nevertheless, home. Even though they'd only lived there for three months, they were set in their ways and followed their own self-imposed daily routine.

Seven of us from hospice visited the first week he was admitted to the hospice program: admitting nurse, social worker, chaplain, home health aide, volunteer, assigned RN, and occupational therapist. We overwhelmed Mr. Dogan and he became confused, almost disoriented. On my second visit, I took a Polaroid camera and a photo album and had him take a picture of me. We put it in his album and underneath I wrote my name, title, and job description. Then I suggested he do this with all his new visitors so he wouldn't get us confused. He loved taking our pictures and interviewing us. It put him back in control. When one of us called to say we were coming to see him, he checked his album and felt comfortable when we walked through the door. He titled his album "The Hospice Angels." He also took pictures of friends and family and added them to the album so we could see the rest of his support system. This simple activity helped turn his life around. He became less depressed and now he had a support system that he could depend on. And he had proof—pictures.

Mr. Dogan was a portly man who moved his wheelchair through the paths in the house by padding his feet along. When he got close to a doorjam, he reached out with his arms and used momentum to pull himself through. His emphysema made him constantly short of breath, so he also pulled along the tube to his supplemental oxygen, trying not to run over it or get it caught on something.

Because of his emphysema Mr. Dogan spoke slowly, as if he had all the time in the world, and nobody's visit was ever less than two hours. After a few sentences, he got out of breath and had to rest a little before he continued. If you began talking before he had finished his entire thought, he held up his hand like a stop sign and you had to wait. He needed to talk about himself—needs, concerns, problems—and he needed to hear about each of our lives because he'd made an emotional connection with each of us. And he needed, every time, to express his gratitude to each of his caregivers.

Mrs. Dogan participated in the sessions with her husband. "How have you been this week, Mrs. Dogan?"

"What?" she asked.

I knew she was hard of hearing. I looked directly at her and spoke slowly and deliberately. "How are you feeling?" I asked again.

"OK, I guess," she said. Her feet didn't quite touch the floor and the couch was too deep to provide any back support. She changed positions every few minutes, trying to get comfortable.

"How about you, Mr. Dogan?" I asked.

"Been having trouble—less energy," he said.

"What are you having trouble doing?" I asked. "Are you still getting real tired using the wheelchair?"

"Yeah—it's getting harder—to get around," he said.

"You want to try one of those electric wheelchairs we talked about— you know, the ones that look kinda like scooters?" I asked.

"What are you talking about?" Mrs. Dogan asked.

Mr. Dogan made eye contact with her and spoke deliberately. "Electric wheelchairs."

"Oh, for heaven's sake," she said, "you don't need that." Then she turned to me. "I don't know why he's getting all this attention. I'm sicker than him and you don't see me in a wheelchair. We don't need all these people coming over, either. He's doing just fine."

"They're just trying to help—that's all," he said to her. He looked back at me. "All this company's—hard on her. She takes—good care—of me. I couldn't—make it—without her." He turned back to her. "Right, honey?"

We tried to include her, but I know she felt isolated because she couldn't hear everything we said. She frequently answered questions that weren't asked or commented inappropriately. She became more nervous and passive-aggressive. The hospice team met to plan ways to be more sensitive to her needs. However, her husband was our patient, and when there had to be a choice, his needs came first.

After we had seen Mr. Dogan for a couple of months, Mrs. Dogan had a stroke. Mr. Dogan drove to the hospital every day to see her, but the stress of this added activity immediately began to wear on him. His volunteer said she would never forget the look of relief on his face when she entered the hospital room and saw him sitting in the dark next to his wife's bed. Overnight, our roles as hospice workers took on new meanings. He opened up further and asked for our help. The volunteer coordinator organized drivers to take him to the hospital, but he still deteriorated with the added stress and activity. Finally, we convinced him to go every other day, so he could conserve energy for when his wife came home.

Their grown children lived two hundred miles away and had children of their own. They called weekly and visited when they could, but it was seldom.

"While your daughter's here, let's work on some things that will make it easier on your wife when she comes home. I know you've hired a person to do some cleaning and cooking, and I know that Mrs. Dogan has certain ways she likes things done. Why don't we make some sample menus so Mrs. Dogan won't have to give the new housekeeper so much instruction when she gets home?"

"I'll try," Mr. Dogan said.

"What's something Mrs. Dogan cooks every week?" I asked.

"Oh, let's see—pork chops—I suppose," he said.

"How does she like to cook them?" I asked.

"Well, let's see—she fries them," he answered.

"Dad, she fries them till they're almost burned," Joann, his daughter, said. "I don't know how you eat them. They're dry as leather."

"Well—that's the way—we like them," he argued.

"That's good," I said. "That's the kind of detail I want to know. What does she usually serve with them?"

"Oh, let's see—you have—to have something sweet—with pork chops," he said. "Cooked apples—yams—pineapples in rings."

We identified the brands of foods she liked to buy. Frozen apple juice tastes different than canned. We worked on this until Mr. Dogan got tired and I encouraged them to continue without me, as he was able. Joann also visited the neighborhood grocery store and made a list of their favorite items in the order in which the store was laid out.

Mrs. Dogan had another stroke and when there was nothing left to do for her in the hospital, she came home as a hospice patient. She was only home two days before she lapsed into a coma. Mr. Dogan kissed his wife good night. "I love you," he told her. "I promise to join you soon." She died within the hour.

Mr. Dogan was able to get a full-time housekeeper and stay home for a few months. Unfortunately, one of his housekeepers took advantage of his vulnerability by stealing his MasterCard and some cash. He continued to trust her because he couldn't believe her betrayal. This betrayal added to his grief. He spent days trying to figure out what he had done to cause this. He discussed the situation with each of his caregivers, hoping for insight. "How could I have been so wrong about judging her character?" he asked. "How could she tell me that she's a Christian, pray with me, and then steal behind my back?"

After Mr. Dogan's wife died, his hospice workers became his extended family. He knew and trusted us. He was closest to his volunteer, Cathy, who lived nearby, was available by phone daily, and visited several times a week. Her husband and children became involved in Mr. Dogan's life, too. When he needed household repairs, Cathy's husband took care of them. The children brought him pictures they'd made and became his surrogate grandchildren. With our combined help, he was able to stay home until he became so weak that he put himself on bedrest in order to conserve energy.

Eventually, Mr. Dogan's son convinced him to move in with his family. Mr. Dogan threw a party for all his caregivers to show his gratitude and say good-bye. Anyone who had anything to do with his care was invited including the admitting nurse who he'd only seen once. Six weeks later he sent us all a Christmas card in July, since he knew he wouldn't make it till December. Again, he thanked us and told us that he loved and missed us. He also drew a map and gave us his new address and phone number, referring to it as his next to final move.

Telling the story of Mr. Dogan reminds me that I need to begin with the most immediate need of the patient. Orienting him to the hospice team had to be done first. I couldn't do anything else until he trusted me and his basic needs were met. Often, the first few sessions for any hospice worker or volunteer are spent on developing trust. Treating a patient often involves working with other members of their support system. Clearly, Mrs. Dogan needed to have reassurance or her anxiety would have an effect on him at each session. Mr. Dogan had a sensitive volunteer and it seemed that every time I came up with a new idea, the two of them had just begun that very thing. He had trouble reading so he asked Cathy to read him a book written by a widower. It helped him deal with his grief and loss. Although this might be an activity for a chaplain, he trusted Cathy the most, so she was the perfect choice. Being a caregiver requires teamwork. It doesn't matter who does what to help the patient, only that the patient's needs get met. Often, it is the home health aide who spends the most time with the patient, hears their needs, and provides the most intimate care. Many times I have seen home health aides pray with patients at the end of their sessions, an activity usually performed by the chaplain. A lot of crossover in roles takes place. It may depend on trust levels, timing (you're in the right place at the right time when the patient has a need), or a variety of other variables. Every individual has his own area of focus and relationship with the patient; but the primary goal, always, is to help the patient meet his needs.

Most of what I did with Mr. Dogan was listen. He needed to talk about his past, current problems, family, wife, grief, and needs. He needed reassurance and emotional support for each decision he made. He needed help with organizing and problem solving. Mr. Dogan had been retired for many years and he had had time to put his affairs in order. What was left for him to deal with was the everydayness at the end of his life—the simple tasks that pile up when you have little energy. He needed attention. He needed to not feel lonely. Like everyone, he basically needed to feel loved. ✞

The ordinary arts we practice every day at home are of more importance to the soul than their simplicity might suggest.

~ SIR THOMAS MORE

$\mathcal{P}$our in Water and Stir

Margaret

Margaret was a burden to her family: She knew it in her mind and felt it in her heart. She felt displaced and in the way. She was not a hospice patient, but when I met her, she told me she wanted to die.

Margaret lived in her son and daughter-in-law's home with their five school-age children. The children made her nervous. They moved too fast, talked too loud, and demanded too much from their parents. The youngest ones ran screaming through the house in their game of tag, as she stood paralyzed. Margaret, however, was the one who needed the nanny, not the children. Since she was legally blind, had a stroke, and was diagnosed with Alzheimer's, she required help with her ongoing basic needs. Because of her health problems and lack of vision, Margaret often seemed anxious and disoriented in the expansive two-story house. Her biggest fear was that she would become even more dependent.

It was winter when I worked with Margaret. We always worked in the kitchen, where the large windows reminded us that it was cold and gray outside. For Margaret, it was cold and gray inside, too, so we had to create our own warmth and happiness when we were together.

The seventy-year-old Shaker-style house was utilitarian. The kitchen was organized in the way my high school home economics class had been organized—enough supplies for the assigned tasks, but nothing frivolous on hand. The refrigerator had only a family schedule and medication chart posted—no snapshots of the children, postcards, or funny magnets.

That first day, I saw her leaning apprehensively as if looking around the corner. I soon learned that she could barely see through her big pink glasses that continually slid down the wrinkled skin on her nose, but she listened for clues.

Dagmar, the young German woman who was her daytime caregiver, introduced me to Margaret, just as I had introduced myself to her. As soon as I took Margaret's hands in mine, the caregiver headed out of the room. "Yell if you need anything," she said. I heard her bound up the stairs two at a time. Dagmar was polite and tolerant, but cared nothing about Margaret. And Margaret cared nothing about her. To Margaret, Dagmar represented an excuse for her son not to directly take care of her.

The high ceilings, oversized rooms, and sparse furnishings made Margaret appear even smaller than she was. She looked like she came from a geriatric version of a Lands' End catalog, and I immediately fell in love with her comfort and casualness. Later, it occurred to me that perhaps someone else chose her clothes and dressed her. She always wore cotton twill pants, crew socks, and tennis shoes. She wore soft cotton layers of an undershirt, a turtleneck, and a heavy overshirt or jacket. Her clothes were rumpled and a little too big. Her long white hair was in a braid down her back and always a little messy, gently framing her face. She took small rigid steps and kept her arms out in front of her, as if walking blindfolded.

"Do you have any pictures of yourself when you were younger?" I asked.

"No, I don't know where they are," she said. "This is Inga's house."

Margaret wanted to feel helpful, not impotent as she felt most of the time. I wanted an activity that was already familiar, so there would be minimal new learning. I also wanted an activity that increased her productivity, interaction with the family, and self-esteem. Since our sessions were in the kitchen, we decided to cook. We started with fruit salad. I chose fruit that could be sliced with a butter knife or easily manipulated—bananas, pineapple slices, seedless grapes, and oranges. Stir in a little yogurt and place in the refrigerator for supper. The next time, we worked with instant pudding. Then we moved on to mixes of all kinds—add water, egg, stir, bake.

Once Margaret was set up with supplies in front of her at the table, she just required verbal cues. "OK, the recipe says that next you pour in the water and stir for three minutes," I read aloud.

She followed through with any project I gave her if I broke it down into small parts. She reached for the bowl, feeling all the way around the rim each time she did something. Before breaking an egg on the rim, she double-checked with me. "Am I over the bowl?"

She made cookies for after school, a vegetable side dish for supper (snap and season green beans), and even made lunch for us a couple of times (peanut butter and jelly, and tuna sandwiches). Every holiday was celebrated with a special treat specific for the occasion, and reminiscing about past celebrations. Afterward, I washed, she dried, I put away the dishes, and she wiped off the table.

If we baked, we sat at the kitchen table with something warm to drink while we waited, and talked as if we were old friends discussing our lives, memories, current events, and family. I discovered that the more she relaxed, the more sense she made. Margaret couldn't process information like she did when she ran her own household. She had difficulty finding the correct words to express what she wanted to say, much like the kind of problems any of us have when we get nervous and pressured and can't remember something simple and familiar. If you took the time to listen, she could tell stories about her children, her husband, her own home, her old neighborhood.

"Tomorrow is October thirty-first," I said. "Do you know what holiday that is?"

"No, doesn't sound familiar," she said.

"I'll give you a hint," I said. "Jack-o'lanterns."

"Oh, pumpkins. Let's see now—oh, I know—fairies, hot apple cider," she said. "The name? I don't know—brooms. I used to put a broom on the door."

"You're right," I said. "It's Halloween."

"That's it," she said. "I knew that."

"Did you ever make your sons' costumes?" I asked.

"Sheets," she said. "Candy apples."

"Did you make ghost costumes out of sheets?" I asked.

"Yeah," she said. "And balls. And apples."

"Balls, let's see—oh, did you make popcorn balls and candy apples?" I asked.

"Yeah, that's it. Oh, we had so much fun," she said. "They were so cute."

"Who was cute—your sons or all the kids that came trick-or-treating?" I asked.

"Oh—why, everybody," she said.

She had insight about her declining physical condition and became tearful when discussing this. She became adept at communicating through metaphors, if you listened with this understanding.

"She doesn't like me living here," Margaret said.

"Who doesn't?" I asked.

"Jonathan's mother," she said.

"What? You mean you don't like living here?" I asked.

"No—well, that too," she said. "No, I mean his mother," she said.

"But you're his mother," I said. "You mean Inga?"

"Uh-huh, Inga," she said. "She doesn't like it."

"Oh. You mean Jonathan's *wife*," I said. "I can see why you call her his mother. She really does act like everyone's mother."

Margaret's behavior changed dramatically if her son came home during our session. "What's he doing home?" she asked. "Is everything OK? JONATHAN? Is he going to stay? Something must be wrong. JONATHAN? I heard him come in. Where'd he go?"

"Sounds like he went upstairs," I said. "I think he just stopped by to pick something up."

"JONATHAN?" Margaret became more frantic. If he was around, nobody else could do anything for her. This manipulation was emotionally and physically draining for both of them. Her son and daughter-in-law were both professionals with demanding careers. Their children needed their attention. They couldn't be stretched to do much more and they thought they could satisfy Margaret's needs with the live-in caregiver. But Margaret had different needs. She needed the person she trusted most to be everything to her. But he couldn't, because it wasn't fair to him, his wife, or his children.

After a few months, Dagmar quit and Margaret moved into a nursing home. I went to see her once. She was no longer my patient, so I talked with the occupational therapist that worked in the nursing home and requested that she help Margaret with the adjustment. When I saw Margaret, she looked thin, pale, and afraid. Someone had fixed her braid into a tight bun on top of her head and there was no loose hair falling softly around her face. She was in a jersey dress and uncomfortable shoes. She was so anxious that I'm not sure she knew who I was, although she said she did. I heard later that she died that spring.

Margaret's son reported in her history that she had reared two sons and never worked outside the home. I could tell he judged her for not seeking higher education and a career. He disdainfully described her as a slave to her family. He said this without knowing that his mother had considered her life to be a success through the accomplishments of her sons. The simplicity of her life had brought her joy, and she said she had no regrets. What he considered subservient behavior, she considered acts of motherly love.

Margaret wanted to be able to take care of her son. She wanted to continue her roles as mother and grandmother. My goals were to help her fill these roles in the limited way she was able. But when I wasn't there, her family didn't provide carryover into other activities. She didn't think I could help her from the beginning, but she was desperate enough to try. She was gracious and willing, and brave to conquer her anxiety when working with me.

The ending of this story is a modern tragedy—although, for a little while, I got to hold her hand. I hope our time together was as rich for her as it was for me. I hope she got to feel what she needed, even if only for a few hours a week. I hope her grandchildren remember the love she tried to express when they have cookies after school or special holiday treats. 🙞

> *. . . in a time lacking in truth and certainty*
> *and filled with anguish and despair,*
> *no woman should be shamefaced in*
> *attempting to give back to the world, through*
> *her work, a portion of its lost heart.*
>
> ～ LOUISE BOGAN

"*L*et's Don't Do Anything Today"

Paloma

> *After the funeral, I packed up her clothing in*
> *boxes destined for Goodwill. "I can't do it," my*
> *father had said, calling from his office*
> *one morning in late July. "Can you please?" I did*
> *it that afternoon when no one else was home,*
> *and I did it deliberately and mechanically, care-*
> *fully unfolding and refolding each sweater, wait-*
> *ing for the good-bye note she never*
> *wrote to flutter to the floor.*
>
> ～ HOPE EDELMAN,
> *Motherless Daughters*

"Let's don't do anything today," Paloma said.

I knew that really meant *I'm not ready*. I respected her wishes and pushed a little at the same time. "OK. Let's just talk about it. Remember, I'll help you. When you're finished, you'll have given them the most perfect gifts, and you won't have to think about it anymore. You'll have given them something of yourself that they'll receive in the future, and that they'll have all of their lives to read whenever they need."

Paloma's main goal was to leave something for her children. She put together a photo album of her history, including pictures of relatives in Spain from where she had moved when she was only eighteen, twenty-two years ago. She wanted her children to have it if they ever became interested in knowing more about her life. Her children were young, ages twelve and ten, and they had no interest in the album now. She also wanted to leave them something more intimate, so she chose to write letters to each of them. Making the decision was the first step, but it was difficult to carry out. It took several more sessions before she was ready. She required emotional support, lots of encouragement, and guidance on how to start.

"What do you most want to tell your children?" I asked. "How do you feel about each child individually? How do you want them to remember you? Is there something you can say to help them cope after you've died? What influence do you want to have on their futures? Just think about it. You don't have to answer today."

Paloma's room was spacious, sensual, and homey. It was a quiet space, separated from the rest of the house. Everything she needed was there, and the kitchen was just next door. She had a large walk-in closet, full bathroom, large windows, and a door to the backyard. The most interesting thing about the room was the presence of the angels, a hundred of them—ceramic, cloth, wood, all different. Her best friend in California sent them to keep her company. They transformed the room into a sacred space. I only saw her go into the rest of the house past the kitchen once, to check on the laundry. She glanced into her children's rooms. It was too much, too stimulating; she rolled her eyes at their messes she didn't have energy to clean up. It was a reality she was pulling away from.

She always received her guests from her bed. "Get into bed with me if you'll be more comfortable or pull the chair a little closer so we can talk while I rest," she said. She moved around until she found a comfortable spot. She had about a dozen pillows in her king-size bed and she not only used the pillows for positioning her body, but also as a work surface. She made an office in her bed by stacking up pillows and spreading out files, papers, or photos. When I visited, I taught her to position her swollen arm (a result of breast cancer) so her hand was a little above her elbow. I also suggested that when she was resting, she position her entire arm on a pillow a little above her heart. These positions encouraged a little more circulation; but, because the swelling was so severe, it made very little visual difference. However, this simple gesture of making sure she was positioned correctly seemed to give her more comfort and confidence when receiving visitors. At least she knew where her arm was (it often felt numb to her) and that it wasn't hanging down with her fingers collecting more and more fluid.

I wanted to climb into bed with her and experience her day as she did, including all the joy and pain. There was a fullness to her life I wanted to learn. I never wanted to leave her at the end of our sessions. But I don't think anyone else wanted to leave, either, and we had to remember to take turns as she taught us her lessons.

I wondered what she looked like before the cortisone puffed her up. She was such a tiny little thing, her curly hair cropped short. Had she always worn it like this or was it growing out from chemotherapy? Her playful and inquisitive eyes gave you the feeling that she was more interested in hearing your story than telling hers. But her face, abdomen, and arm seemed blown out of proportion to the rest of her body. Her right arm was two to three times the size of her left arm. She had to adapt to this and to her lightheadedness when she walked. She always looked a little off-balance, sometimes cradling her right arm in her left as she moved.

She walked as though her shoes were too tight and she couldn't get the wide base of support underneath her that she needed.

I imagined her as a ball of energy, darting back and forth throughout the house before she got sick—checking on the kids' homework, cooking, doing a million things at once. She was still feisty in thought, although no longer in action. Now, she held on to the door molding as she tentatively stepped down the single step between the bedroom and kitchen. She had just enough energy to slowly walk to the stove for a taste of potato soup. She lifted the wooden spoon to her lips, then gave instructions to Angela, her aide, and slowly slipped away, back into bed. You hardly knew she had come and gone, but her presence lingered.

Despite all the physical and emotional pain that Paloma suffered at the end of her life, she understood what it was to be loved. The love did not come from her husband, Lalo. He withdrew. He was angry at her for dying. He was afraid of being a single parent. He was afraid of being alone. He felt awkward and didn't know how to be with her anymore. Paloma had tried so many therapies that weren't covered by insurance that they were now in debt. How much longer would this go on, and would he be bankrupt by the time she died?

Although Paloma grieved for Lalo's love, she did not know how to deal with her husband's pain and anger, when he was unwilling to be with her, touch her, hold her hand, or treat their remaining time together as precious. She didn't need to be in pain and isolation at the end of her life, so she chose differently for herself.

"I shouldn't have to think about how much I'm costing at the end of my life," she said. "This is a very hateful and destructive thing my husband is doing to me." Before she died, she told me that she finally understood it was only a distraction for him in dealing with his overall fear and pain.

Paloma created a nurturing place where she received the love of others. Friends, members of her church, and hospice caregivers provided tremendous support that her husband couldn't give her. She learned self-indulgence at the end of her life and let others take care of her.

"Where do you want to eat lunch?" Angela asked.

"Treat me like a child," Paloma said. "I want all my meals brought to me in bed. No more rigid diets, schedules, or treatments. I eat when I'm hungry. I eat a bowl of ice cream after every meal. Take it out of the freezer now so it has time to get soupy." She chewed slowly and closed her eyes as if each bite of her sandwich was the best thing she'd ever tasted.

Paloma overcame most of her feelings about self-doubt, suffering, and guilt that she carried all of her life till now. "God loves me," she said. "I've been shown through dreams that this is God's plan for me. I asked for a healing and I saw Jesus. He said that he could heal me but it wasn't in the ultimate plan for me. So I asked for a small sample and he told me he'd get rid of a wart—which he did. Then I saw him turn and walk away. As I watched the back of his robes, I felt peace and knew he'd be back for me when the time was right.

"It's sad to leave my children and my friends, but I must go. This is God's plan for them, too. I know they'll be OK. It's so hard though. I used to sleep most of the day and I felt so bad before hospice came in. Then once my medications got regulated, I could stay awake and do things I hadn't been able to do. I knew I was still dying, but I felt better, so all I wanted to do was enjoy life."

This is a frequent occurrence that I observed in hospice work. The patient may either be overmedicated and sleep all the time, or be in too much pain to function. The primary goal of hospice is to keep patients out of pain. Because the nurse stays in such close contact with the patient and family members she is able to watch the symptoms closely and adjust medications accordingly. Often, patients quit sleeping long hours and are able to function more normally. The patients may think their health is improving when they are simply stabilized on their medication. But it is life-giving because now they can make use of the time they have left.

"I talk with everyone when I have the energy," Paloma said. "I try to show them and tell them it is OK. Trust God. I want them to know that life is for living—it's for joy, and death is not scary—it's simply a transition to be with God. No time should be wasted not feeling love and joy and God. Not that you have to be happy every minute, but there should be a deep sense of peace, always.

"My task now is to take care of myself. Heal spiritually. Find joy in the moment. Make peace with God. Only then can I help my children heal, my friends and family."

As Paloma got weaker, she began dealing with practical ways to take care of her family. "I'm asking friends to bring easy recipes that my husband and kids can fix when they have to cook for themselves. Do you have any?"

"Do you have a Crock-Pot?" I asked.

"No, but I could get one," she said.

"Well, they're easy to use. You can throw a few ingredients in it in the morning, and when you get home you have a whole meal ready—stew, roast, beans, chicken and rice casserole. I'll bring some recipes. Then you can decide."

"I was also thinking about getting a puppy," she said. "Muffin's so old. I'm afraid she'll die too close to me. That's too much for them to deal with." She had begun preparing for their physical and emotional future, the way a mother does.

"The hardest part about writing the letters is that it takes me out of the 'now,'" she said. "After all, I'll be dead when my children read them. It's very hard to look that far into the future." This thought made her mind stand still for long periods of time.

This is a confronting and difficult act for any dying parent. It takes tremendous courage. Yet, I believe, it is one of the most important acts a parent can do to help her child heal emotionally. Hopefully, the child inherently knows everything in the letter, and hopefully, the parent has been able to say these thoughts and feelings to the child sometime during her life. As memories fade, it is important to have something tangible—a visible symbol of a parent's love. There are times when children (and adults) need to ask their parent's advice. At those times, they can take out the letter and, hopefully, be able to hear their parent saying exactly what they need.

I would love to have a letter like this from my own mother. When I am surprised by my mother's handwriting because I haven't opened her cookbook in a couple of years, I am bathed with a sense of warmth. I immediately feel the tension flow out of my body. Cooking from that book becomes a familiar activity that we share, as I picture her opening that same book throughout her lifetime.

Once Paloma got started, the words flowed. She had spent a lot of time turning these questions over in her mind. She dictated and I wrote as fast as I could. I came back next time with the first draft and she made adjustments. I tried to help by asking questions. "Do you want to say more about this or does it feel complete?" Then I would read it aloud and ask, "Does it sound like you want it to when they read it?" We were able to finish both letters in only a few sessions.

"I wanted some time with my children to show them things they'd need to know," she said. "Of course, that was too hard, too much to do in too little time. It turned out to be an impossible task, but it's what I wanted. I did get the letters done, which was most important."

Paloma tried to write the letters in her own handwriting but it was too difficult. So I typed them on handmade paper with, what else, an angel at the top. She signed them simply, "Love, Mother." When they were finished, we talked for a while about when they should be given to her children. She finally decided that the best time would be on their sixteenth birthdays. She told her husband her wishes, but ultimately left it up to him to know the right time.

Although I am reluctant to give direct examples because this is such a personal mission, she has allowed me to paraphrase one of her letters, in hopes it will make it easier for another parent.

Dear Becky,

I am so honored that God chose me to be your mother. In our short time together, you taught me so much about love. There were so many things I wanted to teach you and so many places I wanted to show you, but there wasn't enough time.

I could never have thought to ask God for a child so sweet and kind to all living beings as you are. Even when you were very young, you were instinctively gentle with animals. You are a child of peace. When I was so sick, you brought ginger ale to calm my stomach, or you rubbed my feet to help me relax. You mothered me when my biggest wish in the world was to be able to mother you.

I wanted to be there for every moment of your life. I wanted to be there to comfort you when times were hard and celebrate each of your accomplishments. I am so proud of you. You had to develop strength in your heart and find your own path so much earlier than most. I don't understand why God separated us so early but He had a plan for each of us. What I most want you to remember all of your life is that God loves you. When you make mistakes, and part of being human is making mistakes, you simply have to ask His forgiveness. You are showered with His love every minute of your life.

If I am given the choice, I will be your guardian angel. I will come to you in so many ways—the twinkling stars at night, the moment the sun sets, a butterfly that crosses your path, a bird singing its heart out. Anytime you think of me, I will be there by your side. If you have children of your own someday, I will watch over them and protect them also.

Here is all the advice I get to give you. Be your own person. This is how you do it. Don't be hypnotized by society. Always do what feels right to you even if it's not the norm. Listen to yourself for your guidance. Second, always ask for what you need and want. You may not always get it, but you sure won't get it if you don't ask. Be fearless about this. I didn't learn this lesson until I had cancer. And third, put some effort into being healthy. Try to eat some healthy food, have friends that you love, and balance work, play, and rest. In America we tend to get unbalanced with too much work. Most people spend too much time worrying about insignificant things. When you find yourself worrying, connect back to God. Surrender all your worries to Him. Feed your soul what it needs.

I pray that you will have a long, happy life. Always, always, always know that you are loved. The love I feel for you transcends the thin veil between heaven and earth.

Love,
Mother

Paloma used her cancer as a spiritual journey. After diagnosis, she studied New Age teachings, sought out the teachings of her church, connected deeply with others, and put her life values into perspective. In the beginning, she followed rigid practices in order to heal her body; but once she received the prognosis of terminal cancer, she let go of the physical and looked for spiritual answers in her life.

At one of our last sessions, I asked her what it was like to be dying. I knew one of her final missions was to teach, and I certainly didn't want to miss out on any teachings from a person who had done so much spiritual exploration.

"If I start acting silly, it's because of the subject we're talking about," she said. She closed her eyes for a few minutes and settled into thinking about the question. "It's easy now to see everything as a divine message. I feel like I'm already in heaven, so it doesn't really matter whether my station is there or on earth." This is when she told me about the dream of Jesus healing her wart. "The only wonderful death is an honest death or 'real' death. It's very hard to die a real death because people expect a nice death. Often, out of compassion, it's easy to play a role, perform for them. The greatest gift a caregiver can give a dying patient is permission to be honest, to be weak, to be afraid. If you're afraid, say you're afraid. You have to continually confront yourself to get to the truth. You have to look beyond the physical reality into the spiritual realm. If a child asks why you are dying, don't ignore the question. Describe what's going on at their level of maturity rather than playing the role of a hero. What God really wants from us is honesty. If it's good enough for Him, it should be good enough for others."

To be able to continue your role as a loving parent, even after death, is a selfless act.

David, a man with Lou Gehrig's disease, bought greeting cards for his two preschool sons. The cards were for each birthday until they were twenty-one, graduations, weddings, and their first Fathers' Days. Each card had a few notes—something he wanted to tell them specifically for the occasion.

Gladys made a video from her bed seventy-two hours before she died. Her husband sat in bed and held her hand while she talked about her life and her love for each family member. Her husband added his own stories and at times, he cried. Her grown daughter played a piece on her fiddle that she had written for her mother.

There are countless ways to leave a "good-bye note." Each gift is as individual as the person. ৸৯

> *No, No, never forget! . . . Never forget any moment; they are too few.*
>
> ∼ Elizabeth Bowen

*A*nger as a Disguise

Robert

Robert met me at the door and scolded his schnauzer before he greeted me. He set his jaw and tilted his head back so he could look down at me, even though he was only an inch or two taller.

"Do you mind taking off your shoes? I just vacuumed," he said.

"Of course not," I said. "I always take my shoes off. I live in the country—nothing's paved."

I detected a slight look of relief on his face as he watched every move I made, hoping I might be trainable. Robert assumed he needed to set each of his caregivers straight as soon as he met us. It's much like a rider who gets on an unfamiliar horse and has to let him know who's boss immediately. Rather than gently giving the horse a cue, the rider may yank on its mouth with the reins or kick it in the belly. Where do you predict a relationship will go if you meet someone for the first time and they punch you out either physically or emotionally? Robert didn't understand—or perhaps have time for—the dance of two people weighing each other's acceptances and rejections to come to a mutual respect.

Robert didn't have much money, but you couldn't tell that from his apartment. He understood design, and how to combine textures, colors, and shapes. Antiques blended comfortably with contemporary furniture.

The Monet print that hung over the couch softened the room and tied it all together.

His numerous spices were displayed in matching glass vials in the kitchen. Exotic coffees, herbal teas, and imported jams lined up in little rows for viewing. All of his tools were on display, with cooking utensils and pots hanging overhead, and the latest Black & Decker appliances on the counter. Baskets hung from the ceiling with a backdrop of French doors. On the dining table, a wooden bowl held imported chocolates, fresh baked muffins, and bakery cookies. The coffeepot was always on. I wanted to ask him to cook for me, but never did.

Robert created a home with the illusion that an entire family lived there. Framed pictures of past friends sat on every available surface. More food than one person could eat filled the narrow shelves and hanging wire baskets. Notes scattered on the refrigerator door were reminders for him, but they could have been notes to other family members, if there had been any. Each time I visited, there was something new.

"This pillow is beautiful," I said. "You have such good taste. It wasn't here last week, was it?"

"No, just got it yesterday," he said. "John told me I need to stop spending so much. But I found it on sale and I knew it would be perfect for that chair. It's none of his damn business anyway."

"Oh, you're just nesting," I said.

"What do you mean?" he asked.

"My guess is that you want your home to be a haven for when you'll need to be here more. You're just putting things in order. It's important to surround yourself with beauty and comfort."

"You know, you might be right," he said. "My home is becoming more and more important to me." He latched on to this theory, whether it was accurate or not. It gave him permission to take care of himself in a way he understood.

Robert's skin was thin and he just barely seemed to have enough to cover his small frame, looking more like someone twice his age of forty. His graying hair was also thinning but perfectly groomed. He looked hip and classic in his Levi's, loose shirts, and black loafers. His clothes fit in such a way that he looked stylishly thin rather than the emaciated person with AIDS that he was. He was never overdressed. Never slouchy. Perfectly Robert.

He didn't move mechanically, but with caution. He had lost fluidity and spontaneity when he walked, and when he sat down, he wound up like a top. His right arm crossed over at his waist to cradle the elbow of his left arm that kept his cigarette held high, a few inches from his mouth. He snapped the cigarette out of his mouth dramatically as he sat in rigid poses. His jaw was tight. His crossed legs might imply that he was relaxed, but if you looked closely you saw his foot slightly kicking back and forth in a nervous gesture. Tense, he burned up a lot of calories just sitting.

Robert had an electrical storm of conflict in his head, carried in the tight body that he wore like an impenetrable suit. He had a crippling compulsion. He had an urgency to do everything—now and perfectly. It ate away at him. After he got to know me better, he was able to talk about the compulsion.

"My parents divorced when I was three, and my mother got remarried when I was five. My new stepfather was a military man—very serious. Wanted to make a man out of me—said he never liked little, whiny kids. After that, all I remember was getting beaten on a regular basis. I guess Mother wanted to please him—looking back, she might have been afraid of him, too. But she always went along with everything he did to me. I tried to win her love back by pleasing him; but no matter what I did, it was never good enough. Now it seems I had two strangers for parents."

Robert continued to set up similar relationships throughout his life. "This is the fifth time today I've raked these footprints out of this carpet," he said, looking faint with exhaustion. "But you should have met my last roommate. I looked like a pig next to him."

Perfect would never have been good enough for Robert. There was no escape. No feeling good.

"I'm a loner," Robert said. "Others don't live up to my standards. I'm more creative when I'm alone."

Robert yearned to feel some relief, freedom, and casualness. He read self-help books, looking for simplicity and symbolism. His favorite was Shakti Gawain's *Creative Visualization*. I used biofeedback to show him he could have some control over the constant level of tension in his body. We worked on more relaxed ways to sit, and ways of smoking that required less energy. Not only did he learn to do this, he had fun in the process once he realized that a relaxed posture could be more power-ful than a tense one. As he relaxed more, he sometimes gestured more spontaneously.

Some days he unlocked the front door for me and headed straight to the kitchen.

"I've got to calm down. Mind if I smoke?" He lit a cigarette and poured a cup of coffee, not waiting for my reply.

Robert wasn't a person that needed a little push. He needed under-standing and acceptance. He also needed to feel in control of the session. Initially, he almost always chose biofeedback. He listened to relaxation tapes almost daily, which gave him longer periods of respite from the burdens he carried. I only made the tapes available; there were no assign-ments to listen to them.

A few times when I visited, he was tired from the extreme diarrhea that can be a common symptom of AIDS. On those days, we talked about his week, how to simplify his life, how to conserve energy, or how to get more help if he needed it. At times he would lie down and I'd lead him through a guided meditation until he fell asleep.

After a couple of months, Robert was feeling weak and decided he wanted to exercise. I designed a program that progressed slowly. I care-fully monitored it to be energizing rather than draining. He never worked to fatigue; instead, we took long breaks between sets of exercises and talked about other aspects of a healthy lifestyle. We also talked about conserving energy in less important areas of his life so he had more energy for areas that really mattered to him. Some days, compulsion won out and he went through his rituals, like raking the carpet; but other times he was able to save the energy to take his dog for a longer walk or visit an antique store.

Sometimes he just needed to vent. I listened to him rant and rave and watched him pace back and forth. Veins bulged in his neck and temples underneath his transparent skin. I tried to feel what was behind his anger. After he had talked as long as he needed, I tried to say something unobtrusive to reframe his bad feelings.

"Gee, Robert, what you call anger seems like out-of-control pain to me. You say you're a terrible person, but I never feel that's true. Just seems like pain to me." If I felt I could get away with it, I might add, "When I'm with you, I always feel I'm with a really kind and loving, spiritual person. Nobody's kind and loving all the time, but that's who I believe you *really* are." Some days I could see in his eyes that for a little while he believed it, too. Since he liked to read spiritual books, I always tried at these times to relate to his spiritual side. I didn't try to fix things or analyze his behavior; I just told him how I felt. If I could listen gently enough, he usually softened in response and we both glimpsed the "worthy, loving, spiritual" individual that I saw in him.

A few months after I met him, he enrolled in a community college and mapped out plans to get a degree in nutrition, with a minor in chemistry. He bought a desk and organized it with all the perfect accessories. He made it a beautiful, inviting space. I thought he would enjoy the classes, but studying seemed too heavy a burden. It was difficult for Robert to focus on one task in therapy for fifteen minutes, and I wondered how he would handle the stress of deadlines and tests.

"I've always been interested in cooking and nutrition," he said. "It's the key to health, you know. If people just ate right, they wouldn't have so many health problems."

"Yeah, I agree," I said. "You applied to this program three months ago. I know you've been feeling tired lately. Do you still feel up to going this semester?"

"I know it'll be hard, but I think I can do it," he said. "I want to help other people with AIDS. If I'm going to give anything back to the world, this is the way I want to do it."

I agreed to help. We worked on managing stress and time, setting priorities (he still felt the urgency to do everything—*now*), simplifying his life in other areas, and getting some kind of balance of rest, work, and play.

He tried to attend the scheduled lectures but began having diarrhea and was too weak to go, or he lost track of time and realized he was supposed to be in class after it had already started. "It's only been five weeks and I'm getting behind," he said. "My chemistry professor suggested I take a leave of absence. Then, I can take care of my health and be ready for the spring semester. What do you think?"

"Sounds reasonable to me," I said. "You need to take care of yourself."

"I'm not quitting," he said. "Just taking a leave for one semester. I think I can deal with that."

"Go get your stuffed rabbit and go into the bedroom so Jill and I can visit," Robert said to his schnauzer. King Triton listened proudly and attentively. Then he got his stuffed rabbit out of his box of toys and sat on Robert's bed.

King Triton was a little mirror of Robert. He was always impeccably groomed, intelligent, no-nonsense. He got Robert out of his apartment several times a day for a walk. I never saw Robert coo or talk baby talk or roughhouse or rub his belly. He spoke to him matter-of-factly. Not with anger. Not with love. Firm, but respectful, and always in complex sentences.

Robert trusted only a couple of people to take care of King Triton and, occasionally, the dog went for a weekend visit to give Robert a break. His sister was one of those people and eventually King Triton went to live with her—as Robert got less able to take care of him. I often wondered what King Triton's life was like without Robert. Did he get love and cuddling? Did he get fussed over and spoiled? Did he play with other dogs and roll in the dirt? And what was Robert's life like without King Triton? Did he feel a relief—like a burden had been lifted? Or did he miss the constant presence of the beautiful show-quality animal that seemed to live to please him.

A year or so later when a friend of mine had AIDS, he wasn't able to take any positive steps in his life until he got rid of his dog. He worried about what would happen to her when he couldn't take care of her. He knew he was getting sicker every day and needed to be in the hospital. His dog had been a stray that found him, and he loved her dearly but he could no longer deal with the responsibility. He tried to find her a home, but finally took her to the pound and answered their questions as negatively as possible so they would euthanize her. He couldn't bear the thought of her having a bad life and said he felt relieved that she was "taken care of." He checked into the hospital the next day.

As far as I could tell, Robert had one friend left. John lived about a hundred miles away but kept in touch by phone, visited every couple of weeks, and was responsible for Robert's estate and final matters. I met John a couple of times, and he spoke to Robert in the same way Robert spoke to King Triton, firm and with respect. John had learned not to be manipulated by Robert's pain and anger.

"I don't have much to do with my family," Robert said. "I haven't talked to my mother in over a year. I talk to my sister every two or three weeks, but it's usually just about King Triton. She's got her own family to think about." I felt that he wanted to be nurtured but didn't know how to ask, and when it was offered it was so scary for him that he rejected it.

He even isolated his caregivers who had been carefully chosen for him as the most compassionate on the team. He set up rigorous tests of character that were impossible to pass.

Robert asked Mary to take him to a store to return an item. When they got there, he demanded money back for an item they hadn't carried in over a year. He screamed and cursed and caused such a scene that they finally gave him his money back, just to get him out of the store. Mary felt humiliated by his behavior and said, "No more."

Then he asked Jo to clean his apartment so he could conserve his energy. Jo showed up at Robert's scheduled time, gave the apartment a thorough cleaning, and when it was time for her to go see her next patient, Robert demanded she stay and do more. Of course, no cleaning job would have been thorough enough. So Jo said, "No more."

He also asked Greg, a volunteer, to take him to an AA meeting. Greg made a forty-mile round-trip to take him but when he got to Robert's apartment, Robert refused. The first time, he wanted a ride to class. The next time, he wasn't in the mood; instead, he wanted Greg to hang baskets in the kitchen. Greg hung the baskets but, of course, he didn't do it to Robert's satisfaction. The third time, Robert just refused to go to the meeting. He didn't bother to tell Greg that he had had diarrhea all morning and was afraid to leave the house.

"I'm not living my life for these damn workers. They're supposed to be helping me out—doing what I want," he said.

Robert judged others when they disappointed him, criticizing them for their inflexibility when it was he who made the rigid demands. He set them up to fail. It's difficult to step back and see beyond someone's anger when they've directed it at you.

When Robert's life felt totally out of control, he made a decision to enter a psychiatric hospital. However, once in the hospital, he realized there were no quick cures for his depression, obsessive-compulsiveness, and failing health. What little control he had left was taken away from him there. He was very disappointed and returned home and then quit fighting. A week later I visited and he was in and out of consciousness. He was unable to get out of bed and too weak to wipe his mouth. His nurse's aide was from a different agency and I didn't know her. She sat next to his bed and read a romance novel while he slept.

"I need to exercise," he said to me. "Got to get stronger."

"Robert, you're having trouble breathing today," I said. "I'm afraid exercise would make you feel worse. Maybe today you should try to conserve your energy. Can I help you do something else?" His eyes rolled back as he lost consciousness and then abruptly regained it.

"Well, just get out of here if you can't help me," he said in weak, breathy phrases. "Just get out of here. You're no damn help."

I wanted to stay with him, sit beside him, hold his hand, read to him, anything he wanted. But his nurse's aide was attending to him when he was awake. So I left, disappointed that this was probably our last interaction.

He died the next morning.

Robert wanted control over himself and us. He wanted to feel luxury in his life, not emotional and physical poverty. He searched for spiritual answers for his pain. At Christmas, he gave me a children's book. I think he wanted to feel the innocence of childhood before anything bad had happened to him, and he didn't want to feel responsible for his actions now, any more than a two-year-old feels responsible for a tantrum. In all his fury, he wanted to be loved, accepted, and understood.

Robert couldn't have control of his AIDS, but he could control his muscle tension, how he spent his day, and his immediate environment. He might not be able to control his compulsive thoughts all day, but he found comfort in a spiritual reading or a guided meditation. He could have one positive thought and set a goal for the next minute, hour, day, semester, or lifetime. He taught me that people could have control of something. No matter how great their pain, people can draw beauty and comfort into their lives.

I was able to use biofeedback and audiotapes to help Robert deal with his stress. I know that not every caregiver has these tools available. Simply use what you have. If you don't feel you know anything about stress management and your patient or family member wants help in this area, offer to learn together. Libraries, churches, and health-care centers have information. How do you deal with stress? Ask friends how they cope. What is relaxing for one person may create stress for another. What is relaxing now may create stress later. Your main focus is to keep listening carefully to your patient so you will be able to hear what he needs, and then remain flexible. It didn't matter that I had recharged the biofeedback instrument for eight hours, made sure I brought all the equipment I needed, and lugged the case up two flights of stairs. If Robert had different needs when I arrived, then I addressed them. I had to learn to let go of my expectations, even when it was what he had requested just a few days ago. Robert lived in the moment and this was one of his lessons to me.

There may be horrible, vile anger thrown at you as a caregiver, friend, acquaintance, or store manager. It is a lifetime of pain speaking, filled with shame and anger and a longing to be free. It's his upcoming death while you continue to live. He's giving you a glimpse of what's happened to him by sharing his pain, his lack of control at the decline of his life. He's showing you who he has become, and begging for nurturance without asking, that he is unable to accept. Because he gets lost in his anger, he needs someone else to encourage and guide him out of it. If he is not gently redirected with acceptance and loving kindness, the relationship will be abusive because that's what he's been taught. No matter what he says or does, just remember, he wants love.

We're all only fragile threads,
but what a tapestry we make.

~ Jerry Ellis

"You Can Come Around If You Want"

Maude

My hospice information sheet was tucked inside my notebook. I quickly reviewed it, searching for a room number.

Maude Miller
Caucasian female
Age: Seventy-three
Terminal colon cancer
Room 221

I came in through the side door and roamed through the halls, looking for room 221. The nursing home was old and the beige cinder-block walls felt oppressive. The ceiling was low and pipes were exposed, with shut-off valves overhead. Layers of shiny wax made the polished linoleum cold and sterile. The pine cleaner burned my nose, and the smell of sour urine made me feel nauseous. There were people hunched over and sleeping in wheelchairs who were lined up in front of the nursing station. As I passed, outstretched arms with hands opening and closing followed me like iron filings to a magnet.

The rooms fanned out into two wheel-like structures with nursing stations as hubs. The dining room was in the center of the home and divided the two wheels. I supposed this was an efficient design for the nursing staff, but for someone unfamiliar with the building, it was a nightmare. I now had eleven more choices of halls, and they all looked pretty much the same. A resident who is a little confused may never be able to find her room on her own.

I waited patiently at the nurses' station until I finally got the attention of a nurse and asked for directions. She pointed with her pen down one of the halls, as she cradled a phone between shoulder and ear. "Third door on the left, but I doubt she's in it." She quickly resumed her phone conversation.

I went to Maude's room and sure enough, she wasn't there. Then I went back to the nursing station and made my way through the extended arms still begging for attention. The nurse that helped me a minute before had two phone lines flashing and four resident room lights buzzing. She barked orders at a nurse's aide. "Get down to 315. Now. Mrs. Adami's been calling for twenty minutes to get off the toilet."

She saw me and held up her free hand, gesturing for me to wait while she continued talking on the phone. I jumped in at the first lull in conversation. "She's not there. Any more ideas?"

I could see I was just one more imposition on this woman's already thin patience. Without looking up, she pointed in the direction of the dining hall. "She's probably with Mrs. White. If she isn't there," she said, "you'll have to ask the attendant in charge of baths." How to find this attendant wasn't a question I wanted to have to ask.

I walked down to the dining room and saw two women playing dominoes. I walked over to the table and waited for a pause in concentration.

"Hi. I'm Jill. I'm the occupational therapist. Is one of you Maude Miller?"

She looked up and gave me a toothless grin. "That's me, honey. Have a seat. We'll be done in a minute." I watched them complete their game, tally up the score, and pack up the dominoes and note pads.

"Same time tomorrow?" Maude asked her partner.

"I have a doctor's appointment. Could we make it later?"

"How 'bout three?"

We watched as Mrs. White slowly got up, got her balance with her walker, and then stiffly took off down one of the halls. Maude focused her attention on me now. Her hands were full of game supplies so I offered to give her wheelchair a push if she'd just point me in the direction of her room. Off we went down one of the corridors. She exchanged smiles and hellos with everyone we passed. She yelled in and waved to her friends as we passed open doors. I slowed my pace. She filled me in with intimate details of peoples' stories in between greetings.

"Oh, poor Mrs. Reynolds. Her husband died last week," she said. "That's Mr. Jackson's no-good son in there with him. I wonder what he wants this time."

We rolled up to her beige room. Inside was a hospital bed, institutional chest of drawers, fluorescent light buzzing overhead, and lavatory jutting out from the wall near the door to the toilet she shares with the room next door. The good thing, in my mind, was that it was a private room, no roommates to require compromise. She'd left her television on at the foot of the bed and the announcer was finishing *The Price Is Right*. "Foolishness," she said, then wanted to see who won the showcase before we turned it off. While she finished watching her program, I noticed she'd decorated a little in the five months she'd lived there. A few pictures of her husband, daughter, and granddaughter hung on the wall. Her son-in-law had put up a small wooden shelf with half a dozen stuffed animals on it. There was a white teddy bear sitting on the bed, holding a red satin heart that read "I love you." A mauve, crushed velvet, wingback swivel rocker sat in one corner. A dorm-size refrigerator sat next to her bed, with packets of condiments in a jar on top. After the show, I asked if she'd rather be in her easy chair.

"No, it's too close to lunch," she said. "I'll need to be going again soon." An intercom above her bed soon interrupted us with a staticky, blaring announcement that it was time for lunch.

"I'm here to help you with activities," I said. "If there's something you want to be able to do, I'll try to help you do it."

"Oh, honey, I used to do lots of things. Used to do all kinds of things till my hands got too bad." She held up her arthritic hands and flipped them back and forth a few times so I could see her deformities.

"No, honey, I can't think of a thing I want to do," she said. "But I always like company, so you can come around if you want." I agreed to come a few times so we could get to know each other and see if anything developed.

Most of the time I came to visit, she wasn't in her room. She stayed pretty busy, playing dominoes, gossiping, and taking part in most of the nursing home activities. Sometimes she quit what she was doing, and other times I had to wait for her. After a while, some of her visitors wouldn't even look for her. That gave us the idea for our first project—a chalkboard outside her door to let visitors know where to find her, or for visitors to leave a message saying they'd come by. She painted the wooden frame around the chalkboard barn red and tied chalk to a ribbon from the heart cutout at the top. It lent a welcoming country charm to the beige cinder-block wall, and it seemed every time I saw it after that it had "I love you, Maude" written on it. Well, things don't always work out as I plan but I figured all those "I love yous" were as therapeutic as my original intent.

The activity director's office was next to Maude's room, so she was always first to know what was going on. Once a week our city transit system sent out an adapted bus and a group of residents took off for a ride in the country. They wouldn't get off the bus or even have a particular destination. They just went for a drive, sometimes stopping for ice cream on the way home. Imagine how nice that would be if you lived in a nursing home and never got to go anywhere.

Annually, there was a citywide nursing home beauty contest. The activity director decided to enter Maude. They dressed her in her best clothes (a red satin blouse with rhinestones at the neck and cuffs, and dressy black slacks), made up her face, and styled her hair. They took pictures of Maude holding onto the outdoor fountain, with one foot kicked up behind her, Marilyn Monroe style. She could barely stand on both feet, but they talked her into this pose and backed the wheelchair out of the picture while she graciously participated in what she thought was a little silly. They selected a funny poem about growing old for her to read during the talent portion of the contest. She practiced reading it to all of us but could never make it all the way through without laughing. In fact, she always laughed when she talked. It might have been a nervous defense mechanism, but I preferred to think of it as a choice. "I brought down the house when I read it at the competition," she said. She won "most entertaining" and got a trophy to add to her shelf.

The nursing home also had a program in cooperation with one of the primary schools nearby. Once a month, the children made special projects and brought them to their "adopted grandparents." In return, the "grandparents" set up refreshments for the children. I observed this at Christmas when the children brought Christmas trees they had made out of construction paper and glitter. All the residents that were able to attend were waiting in the dining room. The children came in, some more bashful than others, and gently migrated through the parked wheelchairs. The most amazing thing to me was that every child was able to go up to an elderly person, no matter what their condition or how angry or confused they might have looked, hand them a picture, say, "Here, I made this for you," and give them a hug. They were comfortable because they came so often and obviously thought about their "grandparents" as they made their projects. The children then sang a few songs and some of them performed a little dance. One of the residents even sang with them at the top of her lungs the entire time. She didn't know the words, but she seemed to be having a great time and no one seemed to mind. At the end, everyone sang a song together and then had cookies and punch. I was so deeply moved that I cried throughout. I remembered hearing Elizabeth Kübler-Ross suggest that if we had elderly people take care of infants and young children, there would be no day-care crisis in this country. Here was a little piece of that dream.

Mrs. White became weaker and didn't feel like playing dominoes, so Maude began spending more time in her own room. At the same time, Maude was also getting steadily weaker. She slowly came up to a sitting position in bed. She took a minute, as if gathering her nerve. Then she stood halfway, hobbled a few steps, and plopped down into the wheelchair. She used her feet to paddle over to her easy chair. Once again, she stood halfway with her back rounded, held onto armrests and a table while taking those few pivoting steps, and then plopped down into that velvety swivel rocker. She rubbed her distended abdomen in an attempt to diminish the pain.

She moved around until her clothes were adjusted and she was comfortable. She settled in like a queen on her throne because she now had some control. She could see out her door in case anything was going on in the hall that she needed to know about. More importantly, people saw her with her company.

She hid her pain behind a smile for whoever had come to see her. She loved attention. It's as if we were all her children and she easily and genuinely gave out "I love yous," advice, and concern.

"Now, tell me about yourself," she said. "What's going on?"

"Let's see," I said. "This weekend I stayed home while Eddie and Tony went camping. What about you?"

"Oh, same ole, same ole. Nothing much happens around here on weekends. Diane came by Saturday. She's such a good granddaughter. Some of these poor people never have company.

"Why didn't you go camping with them? You need to get out more, have more fun. How are Tony's grades?"

If she needed a work surface, she pulled her over-the-bed table in front of her. She pulled out her scissors from underneath her cushion and was ready for work. It was against nursing home policy to keep scissors in her room, but everyone knew she had them and no one seemed to mind as long as she kept them put away when they weren't in use. If she wasn't sleeping, she was busy. It helped her cope. She understood the purpose and benefits of activity and ad-libbed what I had read in every occupational therapy textbook. "When my hands are busy, I don't feel pain. I like making things, being useful."

Maude didn't seem to have regrets about her life. At least, she didn't dwell on them. She embraced her memories, but her life always seemed to be moving forward from this very moment, full of adventure to fill whatever time there was left. Many of her physical needs were taken care of and routines were set up for her. She didn't have to plan a meal or even decide what to eat. She didn't have to clean house or do her laundry. Even her bath was scheduled for her. She would have chosen to do all of these activities on her own if she'd had the energy, but she didn't and she was able to refocus her energy on creative endeavors.

"We had the prettiest little house, just this side of downtown. Had a garden just big enough for the two of us and a big pecan tree out front. You like pecans?"

"Yes, ma'am, I do," I said.

"Oh, I love pecans," she said. "Used to sit on the porch and shell them and visit with neighbors. I put them in everything—salads, casseroles, desserts. Had a clothesline in the backyard. Oh, how I love the smell of clean sheets after they've hung on the clothesline. Nothin' better than that. Lived there almost thirty years. Guess I thought we'd just live there forever.

"Could you reach in that little refrigerator and get me some strawberry-applesauce? My granddaughter brought it. You ever had it? She said they make all kinds—peach, blueberry, cranberry.

"I remember the day my son-in-law and granddaughter told me they thought I should move to a nursing home. After I got this cancer, they thought taking care of a house was too much for me to handle. I didn't want to at first, but I knew they were right. I was getting run-down.

"Anyway, here I am. I don't seem to be doing too bad for an old woman, do I?"

"No, ma'am," I said. "Seems like you're pretty happy here." A few years earlier, she watched her daughter die of a slow, debilitating, and painful connective tissue disease. Last year, her husband died. Five months ago, she was diagnosed with terminal cancer. This could have easily been the breaking point.

"How do you do it?" I asked.

She grinned her toothless grin and used the old adage, "If life gives you lemons. . . ."

She knew everybody's personal life because she was interested and asked questions. It was on the verge of meddling but she didn't care. She just laughed if someone didn't want to answer her questions. You knew anything personal you told her would be repeated. She lived vicariously in this way and her world became much bigger.

Her stories and gossip were always colorful and I suspect that without even knowing it, she customized the stories for each listener. I suspect, too, that when the chaplain, social worker, her granddaughter, and I all heard the same story, there were dramatically different versions— partly for entertainment, partly for wanting to please each of us, and partly because this is something we all do anyway. We all add or subtract, exaggerate or play down, tolerate or condemn, depending on the listener's identity.

The nursing home went through an administrative change about four months after I met Maude. This was a source of anxiety for her, and she spent a lot of time and energy trying to find out how the change would affect her. Most of what she heard turned out to be just gossip. However, the main part that affected her was employee turnover. Many people quit or got fired, and the temporary employees weren't as involved. During this time, Maude's coat was stolen and she became afraid.

"A hundred dollars," she said. "That coat cost me a hundred dollars. How could anyone steal from an old woman?"

She immediately took action and had her son-in-law install a lock on her closet door where she now kept the things that were most valuable to her. Even as a victim, she took control. She grieved the loss of the coat initially, but it rapidly became a moral issue.

"They must have really needed the coat more than me," she said. The fear decreased with time and she was able to isolate a group of workers as suspects, maintaining her trust in others.

As she spent more time in her room, my activities with her became more involved. It had been helpful to have a couple of months to develop a relationship before she became more confined, so that my coming to see her wasn't a transition but, rather, a continuation. We spent a lot of time decorating her room to make it more personal.

Soon after I first met her, she got a small, potted pine tree that she used as her Christmas tree. We decorated it for Christmas with miniature decorations. After those decorations came down, she pampered the tree continually, watering on certain days, feeding it on others. As Valentine's Day neared, we looked at her little tree and thought, "Hmmm . . . why not?" So we cut out hearts using doilies and foils, and hung them all over the tree. As soon as that holiday was over, we started stenciling and cutting out shamrocks for St. Patrick's, eggs for Easter, etc. It was hard to cut out shamrocks with those arthritic hands, but she became so involved in her work that I had to remind her to take breaks. She dragged her fingers across her knees to straighten them and then they went right back to their original bent position.

We also began decorating her door. On Father's Day, she had pictures of fathers and sons that she clipped from magazines and advertisements. On the Fourth of July, we made fake firecrackers. Flag Day brought an elaborate display of flags. She worked on these projects for hours on her own. During our sessions, I simply helped her finish projects or let her direct me through some of the things that were harder for her. People came from all over the nursing home to see her decorations. Cooks, nurses from other halls, and bookkeepers all stopped by to compliment her artistic talents.

We expanded our efforts to outdoors. The nursing home was on the edge of town, and deer and a variety of birds could be seen from her window. I brought her an old bird feeder I had from home because I knew if she had a feeder, the maintenance men would hang it and keep it filled with birdseed. The day I brought it she was feeling bad, so I just left it to be hung. Next time I visited, that old feeder was scrubbed perfectly clean. I hadn't intended for this activity to involve any work. She continued to amaze me with the tasks she performed with her arthritic hands.

Some days when I arrived she was already in her chair, working. Her arms flew open as wide as she could get them, limited by the arthritis, and her mouth widened into a big grin when I came into the room. She wore a pink polyester pantsuit, and her thin white hair provided an off-center halo floating aimlessly around her head. Her speech was soft and round, in the way it is when people don't wear their dentures.

I often caught her clipping coupons from discarded magazines or Sunday's newspaper. She wasn't cutting them out for herself. She figured that everyone would use coupons if they were already cut out, so she presented these as gifts to all her caregivers. It was important for her to "give back" and she created several ways to do this. She always passed on toiletries (toothbrushes, toothpaste, soap) that charitable organizations brought her. She rarely had a need for these things so it was a gift we could receive without guilt. (We're not supposed to receive gifts but I think if you use reasonable judgment, the act of giving can be hugely therapeutic for the patient.) She knew my husband liked to go camping, so once she gave me a plastic bag filled with condiment packets she hoarded off her meal trays. She thought they'd be practical for camping because they wouldn't take up much room. She'd never even met my family but it was a way to let me know that she valued them, and that I was part of hers.

Maude understood the progression of her disease and all she simply asked was to live fully, without pain, one day at a time for as long as she had left. She gossiped, played games, decorated, enjoyed treats, celebrated holidays and milestones, listened to the news and engaged in her immediate world, enjoyed wildlife from her window, laughed from her belly, asked questions, and really listened to the answers. She talked with her granddaughter every day.

Maude touched me deeply in the degree of dignity she was able to maintain. She had been through many hardships, losing her husband and daughter. When she learned she had cancer, she could have closed off the world and gone to the nursing home and waited to die. Instead, she embraced the time she had left. She easily loved without conditions or limits. She embraced each opportunity I suggested as a way to be creative and have fun. Oh, if I could be so graceful when the time comes.

The last month of her life was difficult. She suddenly got worse and ended up in the hospital. Because she would have to return to the most critical-care wing of her nursing home, her family decided to send her to a different nursing home in order to keep her spirits up. This plan backfired. She was now tearful, demanding, and frequently confused. The caregivers at the new home didn't know the "real" Maude and had little patience for her demands. They didn't know that only two weeks before, this woman would have never let even the smallest favor go unrecognized. When I saw her in the new nursing home, she was agitated and wanted to leave. When I got ready to leave, I reached over the bed with a kiss for her cheek and a familiar, "I love you, Maude." Her response shook me up because it was so out of character from the way she'd been before.

"You don't love me," she said. "If you did, you'd take me home with you."

Well, of course I couldn't take her home with me. But I had to reevaluate my goals with her. Now they were much simpler. How could I make her more physically comfortable? Position her with pillows, adjust the temperature, help her roll over in bed, put lotion on her hands and feet. Is there anything I could do to give her more control of her environment? Velcro the TV remote control within her reach; organize the table next to her bed with water, tissues, lip balm. Remind her of her self-worth. Reminisce and tell stories about things she'd done and all the people who loved her. But mainly I had to remember that no matter how demanding, confronting, and criticizing she became, she needed love and respect, as we all do. ❧

Life is either a daring adventure or nothing.
To keep our faces toward change and
behave like free spirits in the presence of fate
is strength undefeatable.

~ HELEN KELLER

"$\mathcal{I}$ Was Such a Pretty Girl"

Lana

I don't know how Lana used to be, but at this time in her life she was miserable. It seemed her goal in life was to make everyone else miserable, too. "Why me?" she continually asked. She hoped to be healed yet she knew the reality of scleroderma because her mother had died of the same disease. When she wasn't able to live on her own anymore, she moved into her dad's home. She succeeded in making his life so uncomfortable that he put her in a nursing home. She played family members against each other and stayed angry at all of them. She was bitter and impossible to please. So we just had to do what we always did: We had to love her.

"I was such a pretty girl—so pretty. I didn't realize it then," she said as she looked at a picture of herself on the wall. She was embarrassed by the way she looked now. The scleroderma caused her skin to look like a piece of tightly pulled rubber, giving it a hard, thick texture. Her feet were no longer pliable with heel-to-toe movement. She could only walk by leaning to the left to pick up her right foot, and then leaning to the right to pick up her left foot. She made small Chaplinesque movements as she waddled from side to side. Flap, flap, flap was how her feet sounded as she padded along, taking tiny steps so she wouldn't lose her balance. She was afraid of falling, and had to keep the side-to-side momentum going. Her shoulders were rigid, with elbows close to her sides. Her hands were drawn and she used them like claws, opposing all fingers at once to her thumbs. It was impossible for her to reach out a hand to break a fall. She spoke without moving her lips, and barely moved her tongue. Her speech was direct and uncluttered, and her voice was coarse.

It seemed Lana had died a hundred deaths before I met her. Her mother died a month before Lana was diagnosed with the same disease. Her brother died of AIDS. She was divorced. She had been a triathlete. Only one friend came to see her. She could no longer work at the design job she loved, travel, or attract a lover. She no longer painted her abstract paintings or wrote poetry. Her father still grieved for her mother and brother, so he distanced himself from her. She gave up her own home and lived in a nursing home now. She cut the beautiful dark hair she wore halfway down her back in all her pictures. It was easier for the nursing home staff to take care of the short bob. The list goes on and on. Most of all, she mourned the child she wanted but never had.

Lana kept herself walled off from all of us. "I don't need anything today," she said. "I'm doing OK. Thanks for coming. See you next time."

This worked with some caregivers but I usually waited for a second dismissal. "Since I'm already here, let's just visit for a few minutes." The minutes often turned into an hour once we started talking.

We were all continually frustrated when working with Lana. She enticed us with a need, and then rejected us when we tried to fill it. She was thirty-seven years old, close to most of her caregivers' ages. She might have been one of our friends if we had met her earlier. Or one of us could have been her in that nursing home, and we realized that. She wanted to live and we wanted to help her. But as we reached out over and over, we got rejected in subtle, and not so subtle, ways. We had to accept her anger and bitterness and let go of *any* expectations in order to work with her.

Lana had participated in a pain management program a couple of months before she came to the nursing home. "The OT in the hospital did myofascial release and it helped me stay flexible," she said.

"That's a type of bodywork I haven't studied," I said. "But I've always wanted an excuse to take one of the workshops. I think I just got a flyer about a workshop in Houston. Meanwhile, let's see if the massage therapist from hospice has any openings."

After the workshop, I was ready to use my skills, but she only let me work on her twice. It was a disappointment not to be able to help her in this tangible way, but I knew by respecting her unexplainable limits, I gave her a higher gift. She loved Bonnie's massages and by now our relationship had taken a different direction. She wanted to do other things with me. Or at least she said she did.

"I wonder if I could go down to the therapy room and set up an easel," she said.

"I'll talk with them and see if I can arrange it," I said. In my mind, I began designing a splint to hold a paintbrush. "What medium do you like to work with? Do you have supplies or do I need to get some?"

"No, I've got everything I need at my dad's house," she said. "I'll pick up some stuff this weekend." She often went home over the weekends but came back without supplies. After a few weeks, she said she really didn't want to paint.

"I'd like to be able to write poetry," she said. "I have so much going on in my head I'd like to put down on paper."

Her chaplain got her a membership to the local writer's league. She received a monthly publication for support and inspiration. I got her a wide pen since her hand wouldn't close around a regular one. I ordered a writing splint. I taught her how to position her elbow on the table to give her hand stability. We all provided gentle encouragement. As far as I know, she never wrote any poetry.

"I'm sick of watching TV," she said. "I'd love to be able to listen to music." I brought my CD player and let her pick out a dozen CDs from my collection. She let me set her up with it a couple of times.

"No, not today," she said. "I'm afraid the CD player will get stolen. Things like that disappear around here." It sat in the back of her drawer for months until I took it home.

"My hands are getting worse," she said. "I think I need new splints." She had hard plastic splints from the hospital pain program; however, they no longer fit because she hadn't worn them. "I can't get anyone to put them on or take them off. Besides, if I wear them, I can't do anything."

"I see what you mean," I said. "The staff here isn't consistent enough to follow a schedule. How about if I order you some foam splints and you only wear them when someone from hospice is here?" She let me put them on her twice.

"OK, how about just one hand at a time?" I asked.

"No, next time, next time, next time," was always her reply. And I always had hope that next time she would let me help her.

When I ordered the splints, we looked through the catalog to see if there were other adaptive devices she needed. I explained what each device did and whether or not I thought it was worth a try, then let her decide. She selected a toothbrush with a large handle, a pre-threaded dental floss holder, and a large contoured pen. I didn't think she had the strength for the floss holder but she wanted to try. We ordered the equipment and she used it all—once or twice.

At Christmastime, she dictated messages for me to write in cards and she signed a few of them. The week before Christmas, I got a card that she had laboriously written, thanking me for my friendship and the difference I had brought to her life. It was signed, *Love forever, Lana*. Later, I recognized that even though she was unable to accept what she was asking for, she desperately needed it to be given.

In early spring, I convinced her to take a ride in my car. She had a lot of realistic fears before we left.

"What if I get carsick?" she asked. "What if I lose bladder control?"

"Well, we'll clean it up, roll down the windows, and come back," I said. "At least you'll get out of here for a while."

I picked her up in the middle of the afternoon on a bright, warm day. We went to the drive-through at McDonald's because she wanted some soft ice cream. Then we headed out toward the lake. We drove through an affluent retirement neighborhood, looking at the elaborate homes and manicured landscapes. We listened to the radio, joked, made fun of other drivers, enjoyed the warmth of the sun on our skin, and marveled over the patches of wildflowers. It got us out of the nursing home and out of our roles. She was more relaxed and spontaneous. We were probably gone about forty-five minutes with no major mishaps. I like to think she did it for herself, rather than for me.

It seemed the physical thickening of Lana's skin was her emotional armor. The inability to show emotion through facial gestures gave her an edge. She enjoyed playing the "tough guy" when she could make fun of someone or laugh at them. When she showed emotion, it was usually anger, mostly at her father, but also at the nursing home staff. Her father, the one person she should have still been able to depend on, had let her down terribly. "I get so mad at my father," she said. "He's sitting on a ton of money but he won't help me out one bit—says he doesn't have it. Hell, he's eighty. What's he going to spend it on? I get just a few dollars a month from Medicaid. It's just not right." She saw herself as a burden he couldn't bear. She had experienced such tremendous loss in her short life. It would be difficult to get attached to anyone else only to have to let them go, or worse, to have them let *her* go.

"I hate living here," she said. "This nursing home sucks." She had the window bed, but her outside view was another brick wall and a dumpster thirty feet away. The ground outside this corridor was concrete. Her social worker brought a bird feeder, but no birds came because there was no vegetation nearby. She lived in one of the newer nursing homes in town and her room was nice enough. The wallpaper was soothing mauves and dusty blues. The furniture was still new. The floral wingback chair in the corner was always stacked with papers, discouraging anyone from staying too long. There was a picture of Lana with some local celebrities on the wall and a picture of her sister who never visited. An inspirational poem, with a little cloth angel from her chaplain, hung over her bed. She had few possessions at the nursing home. She said she didn't feel that she could take anything else from her father's house, and besides, nice things might get stolen. She didn't feel like shopping and wouldn't tell me what to buy for her room.

As her eighty-year-old roommate deteriorated mentally, Lana got more and more depressed. "She's so confused. She peed in the middle of the floor last night. I'm afraid I won't know, and step in it and fall."

Lana hated the nursing home food and got into fights with the food director. Several times she insisted he come to her room to see her tray, because surely he had no idea how bad it was. "Look, I got spaghetti with ground beef on top but no sauce. Who would eat this?"

"No, Lana," he said. "That's the way it's supposed to be." He didn't remind her that tomato sauce was restricted from her diet and he never offered to accommodate her by providing another sauce.

He left the room and she started crying. "I don't mean to be a bitch. No one listens. I can't get anything done around here."

We all started bringing snack food she could keep in her drawer. She had a few dietary restrictions so we had to be careful. Silver almonds and grapes made her happy. I rescheduled my visits till right before supper so I could bring something she wanted. I called before my visit, and stopped by one of three nearby restaurants to pick up her order. She ate at the beginning of our session, saying how wonderful the food tasted. Ten minutes later she usually vomited most of it up. She apologized if she threw up in her trash can, or pretended nothing had happened if she made it to the bathroom in time.

"Should I stop bringing food?" I asked.

"No, it tastes good," she said. "You've seen that crap they have here. Please, don't stop. I'm OK. Really."

I invited her to my house for Thanksgiving, but she refused because it was too stressful for her to eat in front of others. I fixed a plate and drove it to the nursing home. When I called later that evening, she said she had had some other company, too, and she sounded calmer and softer since people had gone out of their way for her that day.

Christmas was more difficult. "My family all came together and stayed exactly one hour. They brought the usual obligatory gifts—except for my brother-in-law. Look in that bottom drawer. He gave me a cashmere sweater set. Isn't it beautiful?" All she had worn in the nursing home were sweat suits to make dressing easy. With his gift, he reawakened the artist and the woman with needs for beauty and luxury beyond simple day-to day existence. For a few days, she had more energy and seemed happier.

"I'm tired today," she said. "Not much sleep. I have this recurring nightmare about Hell."

"What's that about?" I asked.

"It started when I watched a talk show about people who had near-death experiences. One guy on the show saw demons and horrible monsters and now he's terrified of dying."

Everyone else on the show had had a positive experience and they reported feelings of peace, calm, and joy. Lana focused on the one negative experience and it created severe anxiety that she could not talk about, further alienating her from all of us. Rationalization, stories of other people's experiences, tapping into spiritual belief systems—nothing worked. She had her own demons—something so terrible that none of us could be trusted to understand.

As Lana's condition worsened, she became more peaceful and began bringing her life to a close. She gave away her belongings as gifts, and said all the good-byes she was going to say. At this point in time, what she needed was a sitter or constant companion to make sure she was comfortable, but none was provided. The nursing home sent Lana to the hospital to die because they felt she would have more staff available to her, and they would be better able to control her symptoms. Unfortunately, once she got to the hospital she was given IVs and her life was prolonged another two weeks. Then she became confused and couldn't communicate her needs clearly. When her needs weren't met, she became frustrated and accused people and called them names. When I visited, the nurses and aides were extremely patient and tolerant. I felt embarrassed by her new, extreme behavior. When I tried to understand and fill her needs, I became the subject of attack.

"They're all idiots here," she said. "Could you fix the sheets?"

I looked at the sheets. They seemed OK to me. "Sure, what do you want me to do?"

"Just fix the sheets," she said.

I smoothed them out and made sure they weren't tucked in too tightly around her feet. "Is that better?"

"No, fix the sheets," she said. "What's wrong with you?"

I untucked the sheets to see if that's what she wanted.

"No, no, no," she said, clenching her jaw tighter.

I tucked the sheets back in. "Are you cold? Do you want a blanket?"

"No. I can't get anything I want around here." She started crying and that led to coughing. "Water," she said.

I held the glass of water and placed the straw between her lips. She took a drink and then said, "No, I want water."

"Lana, this is water," I said. "Do you want ice?"

"No, I want water," she said.

"Do you want some mineral water?" I asked. "How about a Coke?"

"No, I just want some goddamn water. Just leave. You're no better than the rest of them."

One day I visited right after the massage therapist. Lana told me she thought Bonnie was trying to murder her. Bonnie, the gentle woman who had nurtured her, cried and laughed with her for months, was now perceived as an enemy. Off and on, we were all the enemy. It made her death more painful for everyone.

The hospice team working with Lana met frequently to compare notes of what was working and what wasn't. We also met to lick our wounds and know that it wasn't only one of us that her anger was directed at: It was all of us. It was the *concept* of us. We discussed if others on the hospice team would be more appropriate to work with Lana, but in this case, we knew it didn't matter.

"It's not because she's my age that makes it hard to work with her," I said. "I'm not projecting."

But, of course, I was. I needed her to live a fuller life. I needed her to not be so depressed. I needed her to not be obsessed with going to Hell. But she had her own needs, so I had to practice letting go of mine.

I never knew what she would want when I arrived. I had to find a spacious place inside myself that could remain open and loving, no matter what was thrown my way.

Lana taught me that every death is not ideal, even when there is a team of us trying our best. People may live and die isolated, but that may not mean they want to die alone. If I had been Lana's family member, I might have deserted her, too. Because I didn't have a history with her, it was easier to back away from the anger that seemed personally directed at me for being her age and continuing to live. It would have been helpful to step out of our roles and be two naked souls. Only this moment matters. I tried to set this up over and over but the closest we ever got was during the car ride. Even though I felt personal disappointment and frequently asked myself how I could motivate her differently, I had to learn that it really didn't matter what I did. When I ask myself what Lana wanted at the end of her life, the answer I hear is that she wanted her family's love and approval. She wanted them not to desert her. I gave her love and approval, and I didn't desert her.

It is only with the heart that one can see rightly;
what is essential is invisible to the eye.

∼ ANTOINE DE SAINT-EXUPÉRY

"Love Always, Daddy"

Bobby

Bobby was as volatile as a firecracker lying in that nursing home bed day after day. I worked with him for almost a year and I never knew what would be brewing when I walked through his door. Bobby was stubborn, willful, and a fighter. But he no longer fought the disease. He knew the reality from family members who died before him. Now he fought for his seven-year-old daughter. I knew that my work with Bobby would center around his ability to continue his role as a father.

Of all the things there were to learn about Bobby, the first thing anyone heard about was his daughter, Kim. "See them pictures?" he said. "That's my daughter. Ain't she cute?"

"Yeah, she looks like a handful," I said.

"She is," he said. "You should meet her. She's somethin' else. She's what I live for now, but I don't get to see her much.

"My wife only lives about thirty minutes from here. We've been separated for a couple of years. She can't handle me like this. Hardly ever brings Kim to see me. That really hurts. If the tables were turned, I'd take Kim to see her."

Bobby was twenty-nine and the youngest patient in the nursing home. He had owned his own home and had run his own towing business, but most important of all, he was a father.

Bobby had ALS, Lou Gehrig's disease. When I met him, he was unable to move any part of his body below his neck. The disease had also affected his tongue, which made his speech thick and difficult to understand. It took tremendous effort for him to form words and push them out, and it seemed to take him forever to say anything.

The first day I saw him, he talked for two hours while I listened with every cell of my body. I got as close to his bed as I could because he had to compete with his roommate's oxygen machine, a loud TV filtering in from another room, occasional crying, and nurses' aides talking loudly as they wheeled hard-of-hearing patients up and down the halls. I asked him to repeat almost everything, sometimes three times. I went away that day with a splitting headache and didn't know how I could ever return.

Because Bobby was young and because his speech was slow and slurred, people responded to him as if he were a child, retarded, or hard of hearing. I saw it happen over and over as people came into his room and yelled at him, as if he couldn't hear them just because he couldn't speak clearly. Or they directed personal questions at me, as if I knew whether his bed needed to be changed. They cut him off because they didn't have time to listen to his answer; or worse, they were able to understand him, but acted as if his answers weren't credible.

Bobby was an impulsive person. Learning patience was an acquired skill and I admired that he adapted as well as he did. He was dependent on others for all his physical needs such as when he ate, how much, how fast, how interested the person feeding him was in making it a pleasant and satisfying experience, even though she had half a dozen others to feed. Break down all your daily activities into tasks dependent on other people. The loss of control is overwhelming. So I was trying to give Bobby back some control.

A yellowed clipping entitled "Could You Just Listen?" hung on the wall in his room. I made a dozen copies so he could give them to his caregivers. I also kept a copy for myself and used it as a meditation before going to see new patients. It reminded me that if I could just listen openly, the patients would always tell me what they wanted or needed to do.

COULD YOU JUST LISTEN?

When I ask you to listen to me
and you start giving me advice,
you have not done what I asked.
When I ask you to listen to me
and you begin to tell me why I shouldn't feel
that way, you are trampling on my feelings.
When I ask you to listen to me and you feel you
have to do something to solve my problem, you
have failed me, strange as that may seem.
Listen! All I asked was that you listen,
not talk to or do—just hear me.
Advice is cheap; twenty cents will get you both
Dear Abby and Billy Graham in the same paper.
I can do for myself; I'm not helpless—maybe
discouraged and faltering, but not helpless.
When you do something for me that I can
and need to do for myself, you contribute
to my fear and inadequacy.
But when you accept as a simple fact that
I do feel what I feel, no matter how irrational,
then I can quit trying to convince you and
can get about this business of understanding
what's behind this irrational feeling.
When that's clear, the answers are obvious
and I don't need advice.

Irrational feelings make more sense
when we understand what's behind them.
Perhaps that's why prayer works, sometimes, for
some people—because God is mute, and He/She
doesn't give advice or try to fix things. "They" just
listen and let you work it out for yourself.
So please listen and just hear me. And if you
want to talk, wait a minute for your turn—and
I'll listen to you.

~ ANONYMOUS

"I know we've just been working together a couple of weeks, but I'm scheduled to go on vacation," I told him during one of our early visits. "I have an idea about something for you to do while I'm gone."

"Let's hear it," he said.

"How about starting a letter to your daughter about special memories you have?" I said. "I was thinking you could tell her things like how you felt the first time you saw her, her first words, her first day of school, stuff like that. I was thinking it could be given to her when she's eighteen or twenty-one or whenever you think would be right."

At this time, Bobby was able to sit in a wheelchair for a few hours a day. He wore a head pointer (special helmetlike device with a long stick attached) for typing on his keyboard. If he was set up correctly and everything went smoothly, he could type one page in three hours.

I visited Bobby the Monday after my vacation. "Find a place to sit," he said. "I want you to read somethin'." He had typed twelve pages. There was little about how he felt about his daughter or his experiences with her. It was a confession and I felt uneasy as I read about his sordid past. At first, in my mind, I judged it. After I thought about it for a while, I realized it was perfect. He knew that all Kim's life she would hear only one side of the story and he needed to be able to tell his when she was older. "Yes, I treated your mother badly. Yes, I had an affair. And yes, I'm sorry for all this."

Even though Bobby had lived with his daughter for five years, he didn't seem to be in touch with the everydayness of parenting. Perhaps he never was in touch with it.

"I remember taking Kim to the grocery store when she was about three," he said. "We came home with bags of candy, ice cream, and potato chips, but no real food. My wife chewed me out up one side and down the other."

"Well, what did you tell her?" I said.

He smiled sheepishly. "What was I supposed to do? It's what she said she wanted."

I imagine life with Bobby had been fun and chaotic, playful, always new and changing. He must have always been on the verge of being out of control, yet able to provide for his family. Despite his anger at his wife, he was also grateful to her for taking over the responsibility that he had to let go of—his daughter.

After he finished his letter, we began talking about what I call a life review project. He chose to make a photo album for Kim. His wife wouldn't give him any photos, so we contacted aunts, uncles, cousins, and his parents. It took a couple of weeks for his relatives to bring or send their photos to the nursing home. Finally, we had a grocery bag full of Bobby's history. I bought an album and we began working. First, he wrote a dedication. Then, he organized the pictures chronologically and I placed them in the album as he dictated a sentence or two to explain each picture. He had complete artistic control. I simply functioned as his hands.

He occasionally worked on a second album for Kim, compiling greeting cards he received. I think he wanted Kim to know that he was supported during this time to alleviate any guilt she might have as an adult. Also, I think he wanted all of our names in one place so that later, if she had any questions about her dad, she could try to track us down.

After Bobby finished the albums for Kim, he made an album for his brother with the pictures he had left over. Donny was in prison until a couple of months before Bobby died and the only communication they had was letters that they sent back and forth every couple of weeks. Bobby saved all his brother's letters and placed them in the album, too. All of his albums were heartfelt, intimate gifts.

When I first worked with Bobby, he could travel with an escort. Just organizing an outing was a complex and draining ordeal for him. He had to find an escort, then coordinate with the nursing home, hospice, and bus schedules. A wheelchair-adapted bus picked us up and returned us to the nursing home at a predetermined time. Bobby had saved money for months, and the week before Halloween we visited a discount department store where he spent all his money on his daughter. He had a great time selecting gifts for her—a Cinderella Halloween costume, T-shirts with tiny bows at the collar, flowered socks, a pink coat, and a computer game. He also had me put a hundred dollar bill in the pocket of her new coat. He used the gifts as a lure to get his wife to bring Kim for a visit. When he saw her, he wanted it to be special. And it was.

Bobby looked forward to visits from his daughter more than anything. It was a time of renewal for him, a time when he got to be a dad. He did whatever it took to get a visit—plead, convince, cajole, beg his wife, his caregivers (in the form of setting the stage), and finally his daughter. Because he was on a nursing home schedule, he had to make sure that he wasn't getting a bath, or having his sheets changed, or a hospice worker wasn't visiting, or any number of other potential interruptions. A complex choreography of events had to be organized. If a last-minute conflict occurred, he always directed his anger at his wife, in order to protect his relationship with his daughter. He understood when she chose to go to a birthday party rather than keep her scheduled visit with him, but he blamed his wife for not enforcing the visit. He understood the possible perceptions a child might have of coming to the nursing home. Just walking through a nursing home to get to the person you love can be scary for a seven-year-old (and many adults).

"My dad was in a nursing home when I was sixteen," I said. "I was older than Kim so you would think it would be easier, but it wasn't. It was really hard to go see him. The worse he got, the less I went. I thought I couldn't bear it."

He knew all of this, yet needed her to have a desire so overwhelming that she would surpass her fear and perform the simple act of visiting her father. The visits were painfully short to Bobby, so each one was planned down to the minute of arrival and departure, activities to be done, subjects to be discussed, and gifts to be exchanged. If all this didn't happen, the pain in his entire limp, defeated body was overwhelming to witness. I saw the conflict in those otherwise clear, blue eyes of whether to scream in unbearable pain, or rage in intolerable anger, or weep in complete despair. With no discernible movement, you could watch the feeling move completely through his body from his now bright red face to the tics in his arms, over his stomach, down his knees to the feet that wouldn't cooperate and push him up out of that godforsaken wheelchair. You couldn't help but share his grief, his pain, his love, and his fear. And the grieving went on for as long as it took. No less, no more. When it was over, the scar would be small but cumulative, and there would be new, bright, blue-eyed hope for the next visit.

We tried to get relatives to bring his daughter to the nursing home. We tried to arrange to have his hospice volunteer pick up his daughter for a visit, but his wife was reluctant to send her with a stranger. Bobby would have gone to her, but his wife refused to let him come home. None of our solutions satisfied his wife so he was always dependent on her for any visits.

I found a series of greeting cards for parents separated from their children. Every other week we sent some kind of "I'm thinking of you" card. He may or may not have dictated a note, but consistently he had me sign them, "*Love always, Daddy.*"

As Christmas got closer, Bobby sent a shopping list with his hospice volunteer to buy gifts for his daughter, since he no longer felt able. He wanted to send Christmas cards and asked me to choose some with a picture of Santa and his reindeer. Knowing this would probably be his last Christmas, and probably his last time to make contact with some of these people, he laboriously dictated a heartfelt note to be written in each card. Perhaps he had spent days of planning since the thoughts flowed easily. But it was physically exhausting to push the words out so that I could hear and understand his speech. It was a simple act of closure. Instead of being his usual open, say-what-you-feel self, he used the cards to make amends, turning anger into love and forgiveness.

Bobby kept his valuables—money, wallet, important papers, and a steak knife—in a bedside table that he had talked the maintenance staff into securing for him. He wore the key on a shoelace around his neck. Having the knife was against the nursing home rules but he insisted on keeping it.

"I keep it in case things get too bad," he said. Of course, he couldn't use it because he couldn't even hold it, but it was a symbol of control, his edge, his right to choose.

At some point, the administrators came by his room and announced that they were doing a room search. They looked through the closet and bathroom.

"We need your key so we can go through your drawers."

"There's no way I'm giving you my key," Bobby said. "This is my home. Those drawers are the only privacy I have. Besides—they're always locked so nothing in them could be of danger to a confused patient." Bobby won and no search was done.

Bobby had quite an extensive love life from his nursing home room. For a while, he had a relationship with an old girlfriend, Beth. They had gone to high school together and when it was time for his ten-year high school reunion, she was his date. He began making plans well in advance, since he was so dependent on others for help. He sent in the registration early, had me order a wrist corsage for Beth, went shopping for new black jeans, a fancy black, double-breasted Western-style shirt, and a black felt cowboy hat to match. He even convinced his doctor to give him an indwelling catheter so he wouldn't have to worry about needing help to go to the bathroom. When Bobby made up his mind, it was astonishing what he could accomplish. Transportation was arranged; every detail was put into place.

I came to see him the following Monday, anxious to hear about the reunion. Instead of sitting in his wheelchair, which was usually where he was when I arrived, he was in bed. His jaws were clenched, his face was still red with anger, and he looked like he could explode at any minute with the violent feelings he was suppressing.

"It was the most humiliating experience of my life," he said.

"I'm so sorry," I said. "What happened?"

"When people asked me questions, Beth answered for me. Not one single person was able to have a conversation with me," he said.

"Did you ask her to stop?" I asked.

"She wouldn't," he said. "Said they couldn't understand me; I took too long to talk. I didn't get to talk to anyone. They all talked to her about me with me sitting right there. It was a nightmare. I never want to see her again."

"I'm so sorry, Bobby," I said. "I guess she was trying to be helpful but sounds like it sure didn't work out that way."

"She wasn't trying to be helpful," he said. "She enjoyed having power over me."

He said he would never get out of bed or go anywhere again. He got out of bed only twice after that—once to get divorced and once to go to the ALS specialist.

A couple of months later, another old girlfriend showed up at the nursing home. I came for my usual Monday visit and he was grinning from ear to ear. "Jenny told me that she's been looking for me for over a year," he said.

"That's sounds pretty special," I said. "What did you tell her?"

"I lied . . . said I'd been lookin' for her, too."

After only a week, they decided to get married. "Bring a newspaper next time. I need to start looking for an apartment."

Knowing how much care Bobby needed, I was surprised. "You're going to move?" I asked.

"Yeah," he said. "Her mom's gonna live with us and help take care of me. They work different shifts so it oughta work out. Hospice can send a nurse out.

"Make it a Sunday paper. I gotta find an ad for rings, too."

He began divorce proceedings from his wife. He picked out simple gold bands. He had a goal and his life was moving forward. In fact, it was speeding forward so fast we all held our breaths, hoping he wouldn't crash. A couple of weeks went by and Jenny came to the realization that Bobby needed more care than could be provided by two people working at other full-time jobs.

"OK," he said. "I don't have to live with her but we could still get married." A week or so more went by and he quit hearing from her. "I can't believe it. She's the one who found me. I fell in love with her all over again."

"I'm sorry, Bobby," I said. "Have you tried to call her?"

"She got an unlisted number," he said. "Her mom won't relay my messages. Says she doesn't want to hear from me. This meant everything to me. You know, it proved I was like other men—that I have needs like other men."

"I'm so sorry that it didn't work out, Bobby," I said. "I'm so sorry that you had to go through something like this."

By this time, all Bobby had control over were slight facial expressions, worsening speech, and the ability to push a hypersensitive bar next to his cheek to call the nurse.

Once Bobby had decided to stay in bed, he spent long hours watching TV. One of the most important things a visitor could do when leaving was make sure he was set up to watch the channel he wanted. One of his favorite stations was the country video channel. Garth Brooks had two songs that were so meaningful to Bobby that he decided he wanted them played at his funeral.

When I heard Garth Brooks was coming to town, I hoped to entice Bobby out of bed by asking him if he wanted to go to the concert. He refused. I called the radio station that was sponsoring the concert and they put me in touch with Garth Brooks's office. It turned out that he couldn't come by the nursing home, but he would be glad to give Bobby a call. Unfortunately, Bobby was in the shower when he called. However, he sent an autographed picture, a key chain, a letter, and a video of the two songs Bobby wanted played at his funeral. We framed the picture, letter, and key chain and hung them on his wall alongside the Lamborghini and Budweiser posters, and snapshots of Kim.

"Can you come at ten on Monday?" Bobby asked. "I need help at the neurologist's. I'm afraid he won't be able to understand me. It'll just take a couple of hours."

"No problem," I said. "You want me to help you make out a list of questions? That way, you won't forget anything."

"No," he said. "I won't forget. You just go with me."

Bobby wore his new all-black Western outfit. By now, there were about thirty pins on his hat advertising beer and chewing tobacco, truck logos, and crude sayings about how to get along with women. He sat in the hot Texas sun waiting for the bus. I'm glad I went because the doctor couldn't understand him at all. We only asked half of his questions because he was excited and spoke too fast for me to understand. I relayed his questions to the doctor as well as I could, mainly from memory. After the visit, his other concerns just seemed to disappear. He was transformed. He had visited with the specialist and magically handed over some of his fears and concerns to the doctor.

Periodically, he received a newsletter from the ALS foundation. I read it to him from cover to cover in search of new findings in research. We came upon an article about a team doing research on familial ALS, the type Bobby had. (His mother, aunt, and grandfather had all died of it.) We immediately sent a letter to the research team so Bobby could be a participant. He wanted to participate in the research to provide more information in case his daughter got ALS. A couple of weeks later, he received a box of vials to be filled with his blood.

It's staggering how complicated simple things can be. The nurses in the nursing home wouldn't draw the blood because they weren't paid to do this. His hospice nurse would be glad to do it for him but she needed a doctor's order. Finally, it got done.

When Bobby's brother got out of prison, he practically moved into the nursing home. "I been stayin' here eight to sixteen hours every day since I got back," Donny said. "Only go home to sleep or run errands."

"I'm thinking 'bout hirin' him to be my personal caregiver," Bobby said. "Nursin' home can't stop me from doin' that, can they?"

Three weeks later when I came by, they were both raging. "Two nurses' aides came in my room while I was sleeping," Bobby said. "One held a pillow over my head and cut the key from around my neck while the other unlocked the drawers and stole all my money."

"Oh my God, Bobby!" I said. "What did you do?"

"It's the worst thing that's ever happened to me," he said. "I can't scream enough for anyone to hear me. I thought I was going to die. I had to wait for the nurse to come by."

"Do you know who did it?" I asked. "Did they catch them?"

"I know who did it but they haven't done anything yet," he said. "I told the administrator they better not ever come near my room again or I'll slap this place with a lawsuit so fast. . . ."

Even though Bobby tended to exaggerate, the administrators treated this incident seriously. Bobby threatened to call TV stations and talked about moving to another nursing home. The whole place was in an uproar. The aides were moved to another floor but the accusations could not be proven. After a few days of extra attention, the talk died down.

A year later I was having lunch with someone who worked at the nursing home. She told me that she heard Bobby's brother had been the one who put the pillow over his head and stole the money. We'll never know what happened but there was always a lot of drama around Bobby, which only increased when his brother was with him.

They both got on each other's nerves more and more as time passed. One day after the first of the month, Donny went to cash Bobby's check for him, but he took the money and disappeared. Bobby was steaming when I arrived. "Take the key to my bedside table," he said. "Get his parole officer's phone number out of my wallet. Go down to the nurse's station. They'll let you use the phone. I'm not lettin' him get away with this. I hope they put his ass back in jail." I didn't see Donny again until the day before Bobby died.

Bobby relived the past with stories of who he had been when he was well, often embellishing to fit the audience. He took pride in his accomplishments, and he needed others to relate to, and understand him—as he had been before all this happened. He needed to hear the respect in our voices.

"I stopped a burglary in progress once," he said. "I was sittin' in my tow truck in a vacant lot 'cross the street, waitin' on my next call. Watched this guy go into a convenience store. Somethin' 'bout him looked wrong.

He was lookin' all around but he didn't see me. I'd been tryin' to snooze, all hunched down in the seat. I radioed in to the cops. They caught him right as he was takin' off."

Bobby agreed to use a communication board the last few months of his life because he was unable to get his needs met when the nurses' aides buzzed in and out of his room. Just about the time one of the aides began to understand him, he or she would quit or be transferred to another unit. He needed a quick, easy means of communication. Since he now stayed in bed and was no longer able to use the head pointer, he used a board that only required him to blink, nod, or make a sound. The board consisted of a grid with a row across the top (A,B,C,D,E,F) and a column down the side (1,2,3,4,5,6). The grid was filled in with items or services that Bobby frequently needed. The aide simply pointed across the top and down the side until Bobby indicated the message he needed to communicate. He also had an alphabet board to communicate needs that weren't listed.

When Bobby got his last check about two weeks before he died, he ordered food from his favorite restaurants and had it delivered to his room each evening.

"What do you order?" I asked.

"Last night I had lobster and shrimp; night before I had pepperoni pizza; tonight I'm having a cheeseburger."

"I know you've been having trouble swallowing," I said. "Are you able to eat OK?"

"I just take a few bites," he said. "Give the rest away." His eyes gestured toward his roommate. "Clarence over there's been gettin' pretty lucky. I figure I deserve a few good 'last' meals after a year and a half in this place."

Although he had extreme limitations, Bobby was able to accomplish a lot during the last year of his life. He achieved spiritual insight that he might not have sought if he hadn't gotten the disease. He made peace with the world, contributed to medical research, left a legacy for his daughter— and he continued to live life, participate in relationships, and have some fun along the way.

Bobby was brave to face his mortality, fears, hopes, and regrets and to make them known to his daughter. He hoped that one day she would understand how much he loved her. While he was still able to sit up in his wheelchair, he also wrote his own obituary and funeral. He explained that the last couple of years had not been as bad as they looked, thanked people individually and collectively, and asked us to help his ex-wife raise his daughter. He even threw in a joke while he had us all together. It was simple, it was loving, and it was Bobby at his highest. We all sang together and cried together and thanked God for giving us Bobby.

"You know, to get this disease really ain't that bad to me. It was harder on you than on me because I felt I was hurting you and never worried about myself 'cause I knew what was in store for me and worked hard to get my reward. . . . I don't want anyone feeling sorry because they couldn't handle me as I was 'cause I was the same way with Aunt Barbara and I understand and forgive you, so don't torture yourself. . . . Well, that's about it. Oh, yeah, Dad and Aunt Mil, I found out that they even let hillbillies into heaven."

—excerpts from Bobby's funeral

*I am not afraid of storms for I am
learning how to sail my ship.*

~ LOUISA MAY ALCOTT

All the Interruptions of Life

Buck

Buck lay in his mini-gymnasium of a hospital bed, in a sparse white room of his government-subsidized apartment. His cancer had spread to his spine. He used his massive arms to lift his upper body off his bed with the help of a trapeze bar. Then he grimaced in pain, cursed, and shook his fists. The bed creaked and groaned underneath him. He pumped up the biceps in his right arm. "Feel this."

Week after week I felt his hard biceps. His arms were as big as my thighs.

"They're half the size they used to be," he said. He was in his late forties, but he looked much older, with leathery skin from years in the sun, graying hair, and a full, unkempt beard. His eyes were swollen, with dark circles underneath. He looked like a bull, resting.

"Gosh, Buck," I said, "even after you've been in bed all this time, you're still the strongest person I know."

His personal belongings—TV remote control, pack of Camels and a disposable lighter, plastic mug of iced-down Coke, and an Altoids box of marijuana—were within arm's reach, and neatly arranged on a hand towel that was laid out like a doily on top of his bedside table.

Nona, Buck's wife, got her big plastic mug of Coke, lit a cigarette, and sat down next to me on her single bed near his. The sheet was pulled up and smoothed over, her bed used as a couch for visitors during the day.

"So what are we doing today?" Nona worked the therapy session as an extension of Buck. It was a creative outlet for her as well—an escape from what was really happening.

Nona was small and wiry, with overpermed blond hair. She wore cutoffs, halter tops, and no shoes. Sometimes she met me at the door and gave me a quick medical update under her breath. I followed her through the living room, strewn with clothes and towels, then through the kitchen, with its overflowing trash can, fast-food wrappers, and empty cans littering the countertop. Roaches scattered. Other times she hollered for me to let myself in. She looked strung out on cigarettes, caffeine, and not enough sleep.

They treated me like a member of the family. Although they pawned something monthly to make it until their next Social Security check, they always offered me one of those big plastic mugs of Coke and wanted to share whatever they were eating. If they were in the middle of a fight when I got there, they went ahead and had it in front of me. They told me stories about other fights and shrugged their shoulders. "I hate to move," Buck said. "Anytime we'd have to move, I'd go get drunk and get thrown in jail so I didn't have to do anything. By the time I got out, it would all be done." Nona just raised her eyebrows, shrugged her shoulders, and held her palms up to the sky whenever he told stories like this. It was almost like they were telling me about some annoying little habit like leaving the toothpaste cap off.

Their two older kids, now in their twenties, wandered in and out of our therapy sessions, contributing stories about their family or consulting their dad for advice. Buck valued his entire family as an extension of himself. He enjoyed their attention and expected their help.

"But Dusty, he's having a—" Buck said.

"—kind of rough time." Nona and Buck were so much a part of each other that they finished each other's sentences.

A TV blared from the living room. Buck's sixteen-year-old son Dusty watched daytime game shows. "He quit school," Buck went on. "Stays out all night with his friends, watches TV, and sleeps all day. Don't do nothing around the house. I told him he had to get a job if he wasn't going to go to school."

Dusty got a job at a car wash, but it wasn't steady work. Instead of adding more structure to his life, it was one more thing he couldn't depend on.

Dusty was like a bomb waiting to explode. He just needed a safe place for it to happen, but there were no safe places for him anymore. The social worker at hospice tried some unsuccessful interventions. Although I couldn't solve the problem of Dusty's inability to cope with his father's dying, I could try to help Buck relieve his own sense of helplessness.

Buck told me that he liked to make jewelry before he got cancer.

"Used to hammer out silver conchos," he said. "Made all kinds of things—belts, key chains, hatbands. One time at a concert, I threw my hat onstage to Willie Nelson. It was a beautiful thing—black felt with my silver concho band. He picked it up, tried it on for size, tipped it toward me, and wore it the rest of the concert. Kept it, too."

"What a great story," I said. "Seems like I'm always in the back at concerts."

"Yeah, that was a good one," he said. "I love Willie."

"I don't know if I can figure out a way for you to work with conchos but how about working with pliers and silver wire to make bracelets? Or you could string beads—say, make a pearl necklace for Nona."

He thought about it for a few minutes. "Pearl necklace sounds good. Can you bring the stuff next time?"

He worked diligently until the necklace was almost finished. I was sitting next to his bed talking with him and Nona when suddenly he hollered into the living room for his oldest son. "Mike! Come here and give me a hand!"

I started to offer to help, but I realized that he didn't ask me because it was important that Mike help him with this gift for Nona. After all, his son would soon succeed him as the patriarch of the family.

Next he had Nona select a dress from a catalog, and he ordered it for her.

"Now she'll have something nice to wear to my funeral," he said. He was directing his energy to have some control over his death. At the same time he was providing his wife with parting gifts so she could feel some dignity for herself and him at the funeral.

Buck also saved money to buy Nona a mobile home. "That way, she'll always have a place to live," he said. Once he put money in the zippered bag between his mattresses, he never took it out. The money and his control over it represented his power as husband, father, and provider.

"I made this picture frame in prison," he said. He had cut matchsticks at precise angles and lengths, glued them together to form chevron patterns, and made the "glass" from a used X-ray film.

"Buck, how long did it take you to make that?" I asked. "I don't know if I have that kind of patience. That's incredible."

"Well, let's just say I had a lot of time with nothing to do," he said.

Buck had been in the penitentiary twice, but he had great respect for the law.

"If we didn't have cops, people could just come in your house and take what they wanted." I think he viewed the law as the parents he never had. He was like a hyperactive child who knew better, but just couldn't control his behavior. Eventually, he would be caught, sent to his room, and be safe again. I never heard him blame anyone else, or deny responsibility for his actions. He knew from prison what it was like to be stripped of everything, and he knew how to survive long, hard times like this. During those times, he had maintained the love of his wife and the respect of his family and he intended not to falter now.

"It was everything to me to wear the 'colors.'" He held up the back of his leather jacket with the elaborate embroidery work that he wore when he rode with the Hell's Angels. "My biggest fear now is that Dusty will wear this after I die. He'd be breaking a code of honor. I'm not sure he really understands the consequences."

We decided to frame the beautiful handiwork and hang it where Buck could continue to enjoy it, hopefully making it more difficult to be sewn back into a jacket. After hanging it on the wall, he further decorated his room by hanging his knife in its hand-tooled leather case underneath. A week later he thought of one more item he wanted to put on the wall. He used to have a motorcycle helmet from the forties that he decorated with a scene from "The Freak Brothers" first comic book. His oldest son had found a similar vintage helmet at a garage sale and I located the vintage comic book.

On the day we planned to reconstruct the helmet, Buck fell into semi-consciousness. The urine bag from his catheter was filled with blood and his breathing was rapid and agitated. We didn't know if he would pull through, so his son and daughter made the helmet as I helped with decoupage instructions. We couldn't work at the dining table because it was piled high with medical papers that no one knew what to do with, pill bottles, important receipts, and old mail. We sat in mismatched chairs in a semicircle around the coffee table—where they ate all their meals while watching TV—and cleared off a place to work.

"Yeah, I remember that helmet," Mike said. "Angie was probably too little to remember."

"I remember it," she said. "At least I think I do. Could be I've just heard 'bout it so much I think I remember. It don't matter. I know what it looks like."

"He loved that helmet," Mike said. "Don't know what happened to it. He thinks it got stolen."

They seemed calmed by having something to make for their father. It gave them a focus. It filled two needs: Buck's final decoration for his wall, and his son and daughter's symbolic gesture of honoring their father and saying good-bye.

"When we were little and Dad would get home from work, he used to take us for a ride around the block or to the 7-Eleven for a Coke. You remember that, don't you, Angie? I used to sit on the front porch and wait for him to come riding up."

"Yeah, he took real good care of us. I remember getting a spanking at school once," Angie said. "It was awful. Had to bend over and touch my toes. Just like the boys. That wasn't right. When Daddy heard 'bout it, he rode his Harley up to that school to have a talk with the principal. I didn't get no more whippin's at school after that.

"You think he's fixin' to die?" she asked me.

"I really don't know, Angie. He's lost a lot of blood. It doesn't look good to me but I haven't talked to the nurse since he's gotten so sick. Would you like to call her?"

"There," Mike said to change the subject. "Looks just like his old helmet. He's gonna love it."

Buck pulled through and had us place the helmet underneath the knife and "colors." At the next hospice team meeting, the chaplain talked about the shrine that Buck had built to his manhood for all of us to see. The shrine became a focal point in the room. "Look at this. This is who I am. This is how I feel. This is who I will always be."

Buck's daughter was pregnant and one of his final goals was to live long enough to meet his grandchild.

When Regina was born, we planned a session so I could take pictures of him with her.

"Nona," he said, "help me trim my hair and beard."

When his granddaughter was placed in bed with him, his muscular fists that shook the entire bed whenever he was frustrated grew soft as marshmallows.

Regina curled up on his tattooed chest. She let out a big sigh, as if she were safe at last.

We took pictures of the whole family with the baby. He showed his granddaughter to all his visitors with a framed enlargement I had made of his favorite picture. I knew this would be an invaluable gift for his granddaughter some day, as Buck's daughter would repeat and hand down all the family stories for generations to come.

Finally, Nona and I helped Buck make a photo album for his granddaughter, while he instructed and told stories. A photo of Buck at nineteen with rugged good looks and chiseled features, so unlike his puffy face now with steroids, could have landed him a role in *Rebel Without a Cause*. He insisted even old, unidentifiable, black-and-white photos go in the album, too.

"Must be family members," he said, "else I wouldn't have 'em."

Buck and Nona argued, laughed, and reminisced over photos of the two of them in their late teens. "Kids," they hollered, "come in here and look at this."

When Buck got sicker, Nona and Angie sat in his room while he slept, and finished the album for him.

One day, shortly before he died, I arrived to find him "shaking-his-fists" angry. A previous visitor had asked him if he realized he was dying. She had wanted him to talk about it, process it. At first, he politely refused. She pushed him, in an effort to be helpful, until he finally kicked her out.

"I know I'm dyin'," he told me. "How could I not know? I just don't wanna talk 'bout it all the time."

I did my best to soothe him. I agreed that it should be his choice, and with someone he trusted, not someone with her own agenda. Besides, I saw him process his dying symbolically through the activities he chose in our sessions.

Buck communicated his view of himself, as well as how he wanted others to see him, through stories and symbols. The shrine measured a period of his life—his brotherhood. His family measured the same period of time, but another part of his life—husband, father, provider. He had many roles and identities that blended together to define "Buck." He simply and creatively expressed his accomplishments, faults, failures, and successes. He gained control of his environment by decorating his bedroom with his shrine and granddaughter's picture. He made gifts for his family with the pearls for his wife and the photo album for everyone to enjoy until it was given to his granddaughter. He had a need to control the money and be the provider. And most important to him, he maintained the love and respect of his family.

There was a naturalness in this home. Time didn't become stagnant as it sometimes does when you're afraid of what the next moment may bring. It kept moving, and except for his youngest son, no one pulled away. (The hospice team tried unsuccessful interventions.) There were no books on how to die. There were no expectations of Buck to "complete" his life. They just lived in the way they always had. It was a natural progression of events with all the interruptions of life. It wasn't always comfortable to hear the stories and arguments and not respond judgmentally, but what made it rich was the honesty with which they spoke. Buck and his family reminded me how simple and casual love and forgiveness can be. 🙟

When there is no wind, row.

〜 PORTUGUESE PROVERB

The Magic of Creation

Gerald

"*Transvestite*—why can't people just say it without making it sound like somethin' wrong?" Gerald said. "My mother never understood.

"I was towel boy when I was in high school. Uh-huh, I was. I had a girlfrien' but little did those hunks know it was them I was after. I could of gotten in a lot of trouble for what I was thinkin' when I was handin' out towels. You gotta be careful.

"My grandaddy's a preacher. If I went to church, I'd go to Goodwill and get a suit. I'd go as a man. I'm not dressin' like this in the house of the Lord."

Gerald radiated glamour and beauty. His rich brown eyes were painted like a showgirl's. His face was symmetrical in the way that peoples' faces rarely are. He painted his lips with Revlon's Love that Red and wore a hairpiece piled high on his head, with a few curls falling softly down his long graceful neck. His cleavage was painted on. He had the lean, lithe body of a dancer and wore a leotard with layers of skirts and scarves that hinted of a woman's figure, but covered enough so you couldn't tell he was a man. He was happiest in the bright purples, pinks, and turquoises that were in his art projects.

"Used to be I couldn't walk anywhere," he said. "Men would stop and offer me rides. Even when they realized I was a man, didn't seem to matter." Gerald was proud of his beauty, and now felt the loss as his body began its decline. Until the last month of his life, Gerald was one of the most beautiful women I had ever met.

Gerald couldn't sit still for long. He was agile as a ballerina, as he glided through a room, gesturing with his long flowing arms, loose skirts and scarves floating in his wake. He was so comfortable in his body that he seemed relaxed anywhere. He lounged one minute, looking as comfortable as a rag doll, and then sprang into action if he had a thought that drew him across the room. When excited, he was playful and hyper with childlike, uninhibited moves. He smiled so fully that his nose wrinkled and his eyes squinted. He laughed with his whole body, throwing his head back, flailing his arms wildly, and spitting a little in the process. He fought depression with every ounce of energy he had and lived each moment in innocent fascination of the world around him.

"No, I didn't use condoms," he said. "I don't like condoms. I never thought this would happen to *me*. I've always been healthy. And anyway, I'm too young to die. I'm only twenty-one. Only *twenty-one*."

What Gerald most wanted was to wake up from this nightmare. He would still be strong, young, and beautiful. After all, this wasn't supposed to happen to him.

Although he rarely left his house or front yard anymore, he knew everything that went on in his neighborhood. You could see a reported crack house across the street and two others from his backyard. The one across the street looked like a regular little white frame house, except that there was frequently a shotgun barrel sticking out of a little panel in the door where a pane of glass should have been.

"See that car?" Gerald asked. I looked at the navy Ford parked half a block away with two men inside.

"There's always someone parked there—day and night," he said. "They're watchin' the house."

"Who is it?" I asked. "Do you know?"

"Don't know. Could be guardin' the house. Might be customers. I 'spect it's cops, don't you?"

Once when I arrived, there was a minor bust. Police cars were everywhere. A young man with no shirt or shoes was handcuffed. My heart pounded with fear, excitement, anger, disgust, and helplessness. For Gerald, it was simply this week's entertainment.

Another time we were sitting in the front yard, enjoying the warmth of a spring day, when a screaming man rushed outside brandishing the shotgun that I had only seen in the door panel. I couldn't see whom he was threatening as he repeatedly held the gun to his shoulder and took aim.

"Let's go inside," I said. We slowly picked up our chairs and casually walked inside Gerald's house. I tried not to look scared. We watched from the window until the angry man went back inside.

"Ain't no big deal," Gerald said. "He's just showing off for you, girl-frien'. Uh-huh. That's what I think. You see the way he looked over here to see if you were lookin'?"

The short sidewalk leading to Gerald's house—a background for many art projects—was covered with multicolored splashes of spray paint. The front yard was dirt with sporadic sprigs of crabgrass. The house was a concrete structure of no more than seven hundred square feet. The front door wasn't quite right on its hinges. The walls were painted white but now they were scarred and marked. A hole in the roof over the bedroom made the ceiling sag. Later, the plaster collapsed and Gerald moved his bed into the living room. Open-flame room heaters provided heat in the winter; an oscillating fan was used in the summer. The ceilings were low. Windows were old, wooden, and leaking. The house was full of cobwebs, dust, mold, roaches, and trash that had been around too long.

On top of this bleak landscape was the one that Gerald created, and it almost made you forget the rest. The central attraction in the living room was what he called Aladdin's lamp. Gold fabric was suspended from two diagonal corners of the ceiling, creating the long curved "lamp." In the center of the room (the middle of the lamp) was a turntable. There were swirling, graduated groups of cardboard circles painted in repetitive patterns with fluorescent purples, pinks, and turquoises that hung from the ceiling with clear fishing line. Feathers, sequins, glitter, and whatever else he had was glued to the discs. He either played a record or placed one of his multicolored cardboard discs in the "lamp" and the room became alive with magic.

Gerald was obsessed with magic. He quoted long passages from a book that he had since he was twelve that explained the laws of the universe in relation to magic. "The magic of today is the technology of tomorrow." He felt it was completely magical that people could sing and talk to us through the TV and radio.

"The circle is a symbol that means 'return,'" he said. "Did you know that, girlfrien'? Uh-huh, that's Native American or some shit like that. That's why I surround myself with them."

His round dining table was incorporated into an art project, too. Navy blue fabric draped from the ceiling from all four corners of the dining room and converged at the table. Ceramic statues of cats drinking milk held the fabric in place. Consequently, he ate all meals in bed.

When the weather was nice, Gerald spent much of his time in his front yard. "Kids love me. Uh-huh. Most of 'em 'round here would rather be hangin' with me than at home." He laughed. "Some of 'em ain't s'pose to come by no more since their parents found out I have AIDS. They do anyway. Not my fault." He shrugged. "They just come."

I soon learned that when I gave him art supplies, there was a good chance that part of them would go home with the children in his neighborhood. "I try, but I just can't tell 'em no," he said. I also realized that it was a small price to pay. Gerald got the interaction he craved. He was the teacher and provider for the children who probably had very little creative stimulus and certainly no art supplies.

I once gave him some plastic material used in making costume jewelry. I showed him how to make earrings like on the package. When I came back, he had made an ornate cross for his mother and a tiara for himself. He held art classes in his front yard again, and the remaining supplies disappeared.

He wanted a carousel in the front yard for the children to play on. We often sat and imagined this tiny carousel in his tiny front yard. He tried to imagine ways to build it out of discarded items but never had the funds or energy to pursue it. Someone brought him a carousel cake decoration and he assembled it for the turntable.

I never met anyone with such a need to create as Gerald. When he was broke, he made art out of discarded and found objects for fun. He had painted a strand of pearls and a tiara on a cat cutout from a bag of cat food and made an elaborate gold frame out of cardboard. Fred Flintstone drove a Stone Age car made out of two empty toilet paper rolls for wheels, a push-up Popsicle stick for a drive shaft and steering wheel, and a cartoon cutout off a cereal box. He was obsessed with his thinning hair, so he saved it and later incorporated it in his artwork.

Because Gerald craved interaction, we rarely worked on projects during our time together. He worked on them mostly when he was alone and would show me his new creations each week. Time with him could be shocking, playful, or reverent. I could be with Gerald the teacher, the artist, the innocent child, the streetwise prostitute, the believer of magic, the spiritualist, the entertainer, or the scared and lonely patient with AIDS. And I could be with them all in one session.

When we worked on a project together, he became totally absorbed and an hour would pass in a minute, as it would for a person in deep meditation. This helped me understand him better because I couldn't imagine how he had the patience to follow through with so many intricate projects. I saw how his art helped him focus on himself. Until now his focus had been sexual pleasure, attractiveness, and other men. He recognized that the creative process was his spiritual path. His spiritual life was all wound up in his art projects—literally.

His house was X-rated. Erotic pictures of men were everywhere. They would frequently be the center of one of his turning spirals.

"This is the only sex I can have now. It doesn't make you uncomfortable, does it?" he asked, not waiting for my answer.

His artwork also frequently contained written messages about mysticism, creativity, and spirituality. If you weren't looking at Gerald, your eyes might rest on a nude male in a compromising position or a spiritual quote to live your life by. He exposed his life through his art for all of us to see.

His biggest fear was that he would die alone. "Jessie's gone all day long," he said. "You got to work a lot of hours driving a taxi. It gets lonely here. Oh, he comes by and brings me food, but he don't stay. I just hope he's not out lookin' for another woman. A man's got needs. You know what I mean, girlfrien'?"

He filled the house with sounds—TV, radio, and scratchy records on that old turntable. "Don't it sound like I'm having a party?" he said. "Let's leave it on. I like it."

"Could we just turn the TV and radio down?" I asked. "I have a little trouble hearing you with everything on."

For a few months, Gerald and Jessie invited a woman off the street to live with them so she could keep Gerald company during the day. "Jill, this is Jasmine," Gerald said. "She's stayin' here now." Jasmine eyed me suspiciously as she brought Gerald some cooked greens.

"Nice to meet you," I said. "I'm so glad Gerald has someone to stay with him."

"Sugar, you need anything else?" she asked Gerald. "No? I'm gonna go take a nap, then."

After she left the room, Gerald turned to me. "She don't talk much. It's just nice having someone else here. You know what I mean?

"Something's wrong with her, though. She's crazy or somethin'. She's been here a week and we had to finally tell her last night to take a bath. Can you imagine? A week without a bath? She's on the streets every night. I don't know how she was gettin' any johns."

Gerald loved all the sitcoms with magic. "How you think Samantha gets her nose to wiggle like that? She must have some kinda magic goin' on. That's all I got to say. Which Darrin do you think is better looking?" He never seemed to tire of the reruns.

"My birthday's next week," Gerald said. "Mother's comin' over and takin' me to *Beauty and the Beast*. All I know is I want to go early and stay all day. And I want nachos with extra cheese. I'm gonna try to get her to take me to Toys "R" Us first. You ever go there? I love that place. I can spend hours there just lookin'.

"You think we could go for a ride?" he asked. "I don't care where. I never get to go nowhere. Sometime if Jessie's not too tired, he'll take me around the block."

"I'd really like to, but since I work for hospice, I'm not supposed to take patients for rides unless it's an emergency or I have special permission," I said. "Has something to do with liability insurance."

"Oh. Well, can we just go sit in your car then?" It broke my heart that he felt so hungry for a new experience that sitting in the car entertained him. We sat in the car in front of his house for about five minutes, and then went for a ride.

When Gerald came home from the hospital after his last serious illness, he lost the battle with depression.

"Want to go out in the front yard?" I asked. "Soak up some rays?"

"They told me to stay in bed in the hospital. Said I was sick and I'd get better if I stayed in bed." I imagine that he was a little stir-crazy in the hospital and the staff needed him to stay out of their hair. I feel certain that he interpreted this to mean that he might get well if he just stayed in bed.

"But you're better now or they wouldn't have sent you home," I said. "You need to get out of bed to build up your strength."

I brought him supplies to work with in bed, but he never did. He was no longer comfortable in his body. He didn't articulate pain but you could see discomfort in the new patterns of holding, stillness.

"I work with different people in different ways," I said. "I have two other patients that I see just for massage. How about if I just rub your feet today? If you don't like it, we won't do it anymore."

I changed my focus. Instead of providing art supplies, instruction, and support for his creative efforts, I massaged his feet and legs, and occasionally his back. He thought it was strange that I did this for him—I could see it in his eyes.

I'm not sure that he ever understood, but he seemed to relax with the touching. I continued to listen to his needs if he could express them, and help him get them met. He nested in his bed as people brought him food. There were junk food containers all around his bed. If he had felt better, he would have turned them into art.

One event got him out of bed after his last hospitalization. For weeks, he looked forward to the carnival's arrival. His partner and volunteer took him in his wheelchair since he was now too weak to walk much at all. Soon after he arrived, he got sick from eating cotton candy and drinking a sugary drink. At least he got to see all the brilliant lights, the rides he had wanted to go on, and a real carousel.

Gerald didn't see barriers. If he wanted something, he tried to figure out how to get it. It usually meant adapting his expectations to meet what was possible. He didn't have great problem-solving skills but what he had was a great imagination. So when he couldn't solve problems, he began to imagine the problems differently. What a great coping skill. I wish you could have known him. He was a dear.

What was difficult about working with Gerald was letting go of my expectations about myself. While my philosophy is to always let the patient lead the way unless they ask for direction, each session usually takes on some sort of form or structure. But with Gerald, I didn't know what we would be doing from one minute to the next. I knew that his flightiness was part of his pathology. It was also part of his coping mechanism and I didn't want to disturb that. I visited, listened, supported, praised finished projects, provided supplies and instruction, and hung on for the ride.

Gerald was self-motivated so I was a little surprised when I received the referral. My job was not to motivate him but to feed the motivation. I had to be able to change my goals in an instant as his needs changed. I had to be able to recognize his needs and help him fulfill them. It was my job to provide him with supplies so he could continue his artwork but it was his need to teach, encourage, entertain, and provide supplies for the children. I had to be able to accept all the different sides of Gerald and not judge a lifestyle because it was different from my own. As much as I was sometimes his teacher, I had to be his willing student as I listened to theories of magic versus technology. If someone walked into his house without knowing Gerald, they might just see junk. The toilet paper rolls and discs of cardboard still pretty much looked like what they were. I had to see Gerald's world as he saw it and let him know that I appreciated the hours of work, dedication, sacrifices, and beauty that he uniquely created. The magic of creation. The magic of life.

If one is lucky, a solitary fantasy can totally
transform one million realities.

⌒ MAYA ANGELOU

"*P*S: I Met You at Camp"

Karen

I peeked into the quiet room to see if Karen was sleeping. She opened her eyes and gestured with her head for me to come into her room. "Just give me a minute to wake up," she said. "I've been waiting for you." I could tell from the minute she started talking that I'd better get comfortable because I wouldn't be going anywhere for awhile.

We talked for a couple of hours that first day. She complained about how seldom her grown son visited. I told her how afraid I had been when my father had been in a nursing home. She seemed to understand the fear, but her son's distance still hurt.

Besides her son, hospice workers, and the nursing home staff, Karen had a support group of about fifteen women who belonged to a Christian sorority. A certificate hung over her bed, declaring her an honorary member. "Yeah, that's from a sorority at the First Baptist Church," she said. "They've taken me on as a 'project.' Once a week I get a visit. Two of them come at a time."

She also had a friend with MS whom she occasionally called on the phone.

"We used to be roommates," she said. "After I moved out, we talked on the phone every day. We're at different stages now—makes it hard to talk."

Karen was forty years old and had been diagnosed with MS for ten years. She had had occupational therapy before, so she had expectations about what we would do together. She readily answered my questions about her ability to function within her limitations.

"I got these wrist splints last time I was in the hospital. They're great. See? My fingers are free so I can pick up the phone," she said as she wiggled her fingers. "My neck hurts all the time, but my stomach is my biggest problem. If I don't get my pills on time, it takes forever to get the pain back under control. Other than that, I really can't feel anything. Will you do me a big favor? Will you check my feet and make sure there's a pillow under them sometime before you go?"

Karen was fed almost exclusively through a tube going into her stomach, yet she was obese. She didn't have the strength to roll over, and was usually positioned on her side with pillows supporting her back. The head of her bed was kept at a thirty-degree angle because she was unable to breathe if lying flat.

Despite the fact that she had an uncooperative body, she had an extremely expressive face. She had round, hopeful eyes. Sometimes she had the tentative eyes of an abused child that almost cried out "don't hit me." In the first thirty seconds of a visit, her face could convey surprise, fear, apprehension, need, pain, and longing.

Karen had lived here for six years and there was a mild level of comfort simply because of familiarity. She didn't have good problem-solving skills, and she frequently panicked and made even poorer decisions. This was a lifelong pattern, now exaggerated by her disease process.

It was easy to figure out why her neck hurt. I noticed that every time anyone came into her room, she lifted her head slightly in order to "reach out" and interact with them. Her head moved just enough to engage the muscles in her neck but not enough to lift her head off the pillow. The muscles in the front of her neck stayed engaged the entire time someone was with her. Using another small pillow under her neck was uncomfortable so we worked on breaking this painful habit. The first step was teaching her what it felt like when her neck was relaxed. "Relax your neck" wasn't something she could relate to, having such little awareness of her body. She was, however, able to relax using images. "Let your head sink into the pillow," I said. "Trust that the bed will support the weight of your head." We practiced using imagery and relaxation exercises over and over, and she practiced daily on her own for a while. "When someone comes to see you, ask them to stand where you can see them without having to strain," I said. "They won't mind."

Her side of the room was devoid of warmth or personality. Her bed was old and rickety, the dented side rails up as if they actually confined her. The room was small with only a sliding curtain for privacy. The air conditioner unit made a droning noise as it switched itself on and off. Empty picture hooks were painted over. A few items hung on her wall, but most were thoughtlessly placed behind the head of her bed, so she couldn't see them. Karen was always hot and couldn't tolerate weight on her, so all that was on her bed were stark white sheets. There was no color, texture, or warmth—just a pale woman in a sterile sea of white. Despite all this white—sheets, floors, walls, and ceiling—nothing ever looked or felt quite clean.

Someone had taken more time to decorate her elderly roommate's side. Family photographs and crafted, handmade objects hung on the walls. A bright floral bedspread with a color-coordinated braided rug made her side warm and welcoming. Often, I visited around three in the afternoon, which was the change of shift at the nursing home. "Karen, you're crying. What's wrong?" I asked.

"I asked for my pills over two hours ago but all I got was a guilt trip laid on me," she said. "Now I'll have to wait for the 3–11 shift to finish their staff meeting. It will be at least another hour before they'll get to me. I try to understand when they're short-staffed, but they're *always* short-staffed."

"Karen, this sort of thing happens a lot. Have you ever considered moving to another nursing home?" I asked.

"Oh, I guess I've thought about it," she said. "But they all know me here." She started crying again.

"There's some comfort in that, but they also have expectations," I said. "In a new place, there won't be expectations. It seems that they're too close to you to see how much your condition has changed over the years."

"But I don't know if my doctor will treat me at another nursing home," she said. "He only goes to certain ones."

"If you want to stay with him, you could ask him where he goes," I said. "Do you feel like you get good quality care from him? Remember, you're the consumer. You're paying for all this, and you need to make sure you're getting the best possible care while you're still able to make these decisions. Almost every time I come, you're in severe pain. That's not right, Karen. Not when it can be controlled. I hate to watch you spend the rest of your life in uncontrolled pain. I'm not asking you to make a decision. Just think about your options. Take care of yourself."

Some of the nurses had worked with Karen for a long time, and to them, she wasn't a dying patient. Their goal had been to keep her on low doses of medication to decrease the chances of narcotic addiction. It was difficult for them to change their behavior when hospice declared Karen to be in the last stages of her life, expected increased pain, and reorganized her medication schedule.

Karen's doctor had been with her for so long that he had learned to mistrust her judgments, too. Having been manipulated over and over, he was now unable to hear her needs. A simple order from him could have easily solved the medication problem. But rather than spending time with Karen and listening to her needs, he listened to the nursing home staff. She had cried "wolf" too many times.

Karen had come from an abusive family. To escape, she married impulsively. Shortly after her son was born, her husband was accused of sexually abusing children in their church. She fled the relationship, took a job as a bookkeeper, and reared her child on her own. Instead of viewing this as a positive, powerful move, she considered herself a failure at marriage, since she lost the support of her family and church. This was a woman who carried secrets of shame until she was dying. She had little confidence in herself and a sense of fear that she carried in both her mind and body.

When Karen asked for something, she begged in a childlike voice rather than simply stating her needs. She was initially enthusiastic when I asked her if she wanted to learn assertiveness skills. We rehearsed what she would say to the director of nursing and her doctor. She made a few gains in therapy but could not carry them over to real-life situations. It was such a pattern for her to present herself as a victim, her words were not believable because of her tone of voice and demeanor.

Karen seemed as confined to me as a person could be. She seemed pinned down, both physically and emotionally, by herself, her doctor, the nursing home staff, her family, and her childhood from long ago. She was so starved for attention that each time any of us came into her room, her face lit up like she'd seen the angel of mercy. No matter how much pain she was in or how tired she was, she never complained of too much company. She confided in us individually, telling each person they were the only one that understood. She imagined that if she was good enough, we would all like her. Instead, we were all frustrated with her insincerity (denial), the sugar-coated explosion that would never happen.

People do things for their own reasons and what may seem logical to you or me doesn't meet their needs at all. It was a disadvantage for Karen to be in that nursing home after six years. She blindly trusted her doctor even when he was inattentive, disrespectful, and manipulative. It was the abused child syndrome all over again.

During this time, it was difficult to listen to Karen complain. She was provided with plenty of alternatives—different medications, different nursing home, different doctor, and alternative pain control techniques. It was her decision not to act further. I could only make suggestions; decisions for change had to come from her. Eventually, after making a lot of phone calls, she was able to find a nursing home that convinced her they would provide better care. This took months.

At the new nursing home, her room was cleaner and most of the time she didn't have a roommate. Because she entered the home as a hospice patient, there were no questions about the amounts of narcotics needed to control her pain. Of course, she had anxiety with the adjustment but the staff was more attentive and caring, and her pain was better controlled.

"If I could just read!" Karen said. "I used to read for hours."

The only leisure activities Karen had when I met her were watching TV, talking on the phone, and visiting with people who came to see her. The MS altered her vision, and her hands were weak, with coordination problems. She had listened to books on tape but they didn't provide enough stimulation and put her to sleep. It seemed doubtful to me, but what would we lose if we tried? Our public library offered a catalog of large-print books to nursing home patients. She found her favorite authors and requested the available romance novels. Then we worked on positioning her in bed. If she was lying on her right side so her stronger, more stable left hand could turn the pages, and set up with a pillow as a support for the back of the book, she was able to read. Being able to perform this single act seemed more of a comfort to her than any other activity we worked on. It gave her a sense of independence to escape her life in the nursing home.

I worked with Karen at about the same time I worked with Bobby. They both sent Christmas cards, but for different reasons. Bobby sent a few cards with heartfelt messages to make amends with friends and family, whereas Karen sent out sixty-five cards and just asked me to sign them "Love, Karen." Her goal was to get enough cards in response to cover the bathroom door at the foot of her bed, thus making her feel loved, needed, important, and remembered. The previous summer she had gone to Camp Can Do, a camp for adults with MS, and had names and addresses of all the campers. On a few of the cards, she had me write "PS: I met you at camp" in case they didn't remember her. While I wrote, making sure that all the cards had a return address, Karen told stories about each person and the fun she'd had at camp. At Christmas-time that year, her room, full of cards and memories, was beautifully decorated and transformed into a warm and welcoming place.

Years before, Karen's son had given her a picture collage of himself and it hung on her wall next to several other pictures of him. Karen combined the pictures in the collage with stories in a photo album to give back to him. She told stories about the pictures and what she could remember about that period of their lives, and I wrote them down for her. It allowed her to leave him some memories that he might have forgotten, and something to keep that will comfort him and remind him of her.

A large part of what we worked on in therapy was not only Karen taking care of herself, but her need to take care of Kevin—at least as much as a mother can take care of a son who's on his own and seldom comes around for a visit. She said Kevin was angry at God and this wor-ried her because she was a devout Christian.

"How did *you* feel when you first found out you had multiple scle-rosis?" I asked her.

"Overwhelmed at first. Then I guess I felt angry," she said.

"Oh, angry at whom?" I asked.

She considered this for a few moments. "I guess I felt angry at God."

"Yeah? Your son's only twenty-three," I said. "He's younger than you were when you started dealing with all this. Let him know your feelings, but then give him some time to work things out. He's your son. He'll figure it out."

He was also angry at *her* for being ill. But this was a subject she never brought up.

Another activity Karen did in therapy was to write a letter to her mother. (This was hard because she had been estranged from her mother for over twenty years.) She had conflicting emotions about her mother and it was a painful, cathartic process. She experienced a barrage of emotions as she wrote and rewrote the letter. She wrote out her anger but didn't want to send these letters. When it was finally in a stage that was accepting, as opposed to accusing, we sent it. Her intent was to be able to receive a similar "acceptance" letter from her mother. Unfortunately, she never heard from her mother; however, she died knowing she had done everything she could to reach her in a loving, kind way.

Karen chose to write her own funeral. "I'm a little confused," I said. "Why do you want to do this in therapy? It's usually something you do with a chaplain. I don't know anything about writing funerals." I wasn't immune to her manipulative behavior and needed to be careful not to interfere with the chaplain's role.

"Well, it's a creative activity and that's what we do in OT—creative activities," she said.

"But, Karen, really, I don't know anything about writing funerals," I said. "I think you'd be better off working with the chaplain on this."

"That's OK," she said. "We'll learn together."

So we worked on her funeral. I checked out books from the library and *I* asked the chaplain for help. I read passages to her (since the print was too small) and she selected readings and hymns. We collected it all together with specific details of who was to do what, placed it in her Bible, and breathed a deep sigh of relief. She had gained control of how she would be remembered as she left this world.

"Karen, did I misunderstand you?" I asked. "I thought you said your son was engaged."

"Well, I think she's *the one*," she said.

"When I congratulated him, he said he'd only known her a couple of weeks," I said.

"Yeah, but I can tell by the way they look at each other," she said. "She's the one." Karen lived only one more week. She needed to know that Kevin would have someone after she died. I wondered about the stories Karen had told me over the past year. How much had she exaggerated and how different were her son's versions?

Karen taught me that no one has to die alone. She had asked for a community and gotten it through her health-care providers at the nursing home and hospice, a local church sorority, acquaintances with MS, and her son. She craved love and attention and tried to make each of her acquaintances feel they were her best friend. She reminded me to be open to adapting activities, even when the probability for success is low. I really didn't think she would be able to read because of multiple problems—positioning her in bed, positioning the book, making the most of her limited hand skills to turn pages, and dealing with her altered vision. Karen epitomizes tolerance and the ability to make the most of a bad situation. We can learn from her that our goals are not always the same as our patients. There are often secondary motivations that we don't understand. But we must always respect all of their needs.

Trust that still, small voice that says,
"That might work and I'll try it."

~ DIANE MARIECHILD

"Opie, Opie, Opie"

Laurie

Laurie was thirty-seven and lived in a nursing home. Her multiple sclerosis caused continual tremors. Anytime she tried to have purposeful movement, such as reach for her stuffed dog, Opie, her tremors got much worse. Her body seemed in a constant state of agitation, and her eyes seemed tired and resigned.

The first time I met Laurie I knew nothing about her except her name, age, and diagnosis. I asked questions but didn't get coherent responses. I asked her occupation and she threw out the word "police."

"Were you a policewoman?" I asked.

She became more alert and focused. "Yes," she said. Then she said the word "Dad" over and over.

"Was your dad a policeman?" I asked.

Her eyes got wider. "Yes," she said.

There was excitement in her eyes as I continued to guess the next part of her story. "Did you have a motorcycle?" I asked.

"Yes, yes, yes," she said.

I felt quite confident that we were communicating easily, as long as I asked yes/no questions. I was also pleased that she was so enthusiastic about my ability to get information from her. After a little while, I realized that all of her answers were "yes" so I reluctantly asked a question that was the opposite of what I had just asked. Unfortunately, I got another enthusiastic "yes."

Laurie often did something referred to as parroting. She repeated a word that she had just heard, over and over. She occasionally threw out a few seemingly unrelated words. I asked questions to piece together a story and she became enthusiastic and excited. But when I talked to someone who knew a little piece of her history, I realized that the story I just worked out was all wrong. The problem was that no one knew much about Laurie's history. Given the violent nature of the words she brought up, her social worker was concerned that she might have been abused as a child.

Laurie's family consisted of a mother and a daughter. I called her mother to get some background information.

"Could you just tell me a little about Laurie's interests?" I asked. "She mentioned the word 'policemen.' Was she a policewoman? Was her father a policeman?"

"Oh, heavens no," she said. "Her father was a doctor. He died five— make that six—years ago. Laurie studied to be a nurse's aide but then got married and had a baby. We hoped she'd go on to college but she never did."

"Does her daughter visit her?" I asked. "Are they close?"

"No, Annette lives in Kansas now," she said. "She got married too young, too. Now she's divorced. I sent her a bracelet for her birthday but never got a thank-you card, so I don't know what's happened to her. Haven't heard from her in about a year, I guess."

"Does Laurie have any hobbies?" I asked.

"Let's see—she loves animals," she said. "Oh, and art. She used to oil paint. Her first painting was a picture of three horses looking over a fence. Oh, and she loved to dance."

I felt like I had touched a nerve with this information revealed. Her mother cut the conversation short and did not invite me to call her back if I had further questions.

The inability to communicate was frustrating from a caregiver stand-point. It was so frustrating for Laurie's family that they didn't come to see her. As far as I know, no one from her past came to see her. I can't imagine the frustration and disappointment Laurie felt, not having her needs met day after day. Was my guessing game entertaining to her and so she played along, or was she confused and genuinely trying to communicate with me? I don't know that it matters. Either way, she participated with passion.

I brought magazines to look at together, hoping this would give us something to talk about and improve our ability to communicate. I held a magazine in front of her in bed and talked about the pictures as she looked on and sometimes parroted my comments. Twice she initiated comments that communicated her feelings when she said "bad" for a cigarette ad and "hot stuff" for a picture of Johnny Depp.

Her room was almost devoid of decoration. I chose pictures from the magazines that held her attention and started a collage on her wall. I added pictures of horses and dogs. Someone at the nursing home believed that Laurie had had a German shepherd before she came to the home, so I added a picture of a German shepherd. She had a stuffed dog that was always behind her head or on the floor or out of reach. When I handed it to her, she usually responded with a smile and a continuous repetition of "Opie, Opie, Opie." "Opie" was the only word that I heard her use consistently without parroting, and I wondered about the place in her heart where this dear friend lived.

Laurie was never taken out of bed to go to activities, and it seemed to me that her dull eyes needed some stimulation. Depend-ing on her mood, her eyes looked passive and empty or enthusi-astic and animated, but rarely anything in between. One day when I was visiting, we heard an announcement that there would be a Bible study group at two o'clock. I suspected that Laurie might be religious because the only original decoration in her room was a crucifix. I didn't know if it was hers or if someone else placed it there. I knew that the attendants wouldn't get her out of bed for this activity. It was ten minutes till two, so I ran down the hall and asked the minister if he could come to Laurie's room and say hi and maybe offer a prayer. When he walked in, Laurie smiled, became excited, and tried to communicate. He recognized her, too, and said she used to come to the group when she was in a wheelchair. Here was another piece of Laurie's puzzle. I added religious pictures to her collage and sometimes read anecdotal stories out of Christian magazines. I asked the minister to come by when he could. I also requested a male volunteer for Laurie, since all her caregivers were women. I hadn't known if she had responded to the minister, a familiar face, or a man, but I thought I would cover all the bases. I knew a specific volunteer that I thought would be perfect—someone who was her age, handsome, had a gentle nature, loved animals, and wouldn't be too uncomfortable with her inability to talk.

From time to time, I tried to help Laurie with simple grooming. Because she moved her head from side to side with the tremors, the hair on the back of her head was matted. Since her family didn't request and pay for haircuts, they were seldom provided. Brushing her hair was difficult because she couldn't get out of bed, and when she tried to be still, the tremors increased. A few times she selected bright nail polish from the few I brought, and I held her hands as still as I could while I painted her nails. I also brought makeup but no one ever applied it for her but me.

At Christmas, I decorated her room. I asked if she wanted to send Christmas cards, and proceeded slowly and carefully since she was almost incapable of saying no unless she was parroting. I bought pretty cards for her mother and daughter, the only two addresses that I had (from her medical chart). I discussed it with her as I signed the cards "Love, Mother" and "Love, Laurie." She studied the cards for a long time before I sealed them in their envelopes. She was especially interested in her daughter's card, and looked at it carefully as if she was trying to remember something. I treaded carefully here so that I wasn't in the middle of opening old wounds for three estranged family members. I paid close attention to her responses and because the activity seemed to calm rather than agitate her, I proceeded. It was one last chance to reach out.

Even though it was almost impossible to communicate with Laurie, there were small, simple things that we could relate about. It was more difficult for me to work with her because I didn't have the usual cues that I draw from—a social history, verbal communication, body language, or environment. The one family member that I talked with wasn't very forthcoming. Turnover at the nursing home was frequent, so facts were passed down as rumors and could not be considered accurate. I tried to provide her with company, gentle support, and enrichment of her world from a nursing home bed. 🙟

True life is lived when tiny changes occur.

∼ Leo Tolstoy

$\mathcal{T}$he Matriarch

Rosa

The gate hung by its bottom hinge, so you had to lift it open. The yard was mostly dirt, shaded by two pecan trees. Potted plants were grouped together like a tiny tropical forest where the sun laced through the trees. A cracked sidewalk led to the stacked cinder blocks used for uneven stairs into the house. A crocheted angel hung as a curtain in the window of the crooked, peeling front door; and the screen door had a new spring so it slammed behind you, like a spanking. The house was a long, narrow maze and my destination was always the last room.

Usually, no one answered my knock, so I let myself into the front room furnished only with an industrial-type sewing machine, an ironing board, and a rocking chair. I gently knocked on the bedroom door. Most of the time, the bedroom was filled with one or more sleeping occupants who didn't want to be awakened, no matter what time of day. I tiptoed over yesterday's clothes or sleeping bodies to get to the kitchen. Once I got there, I began calling Rosa's name so I didn't appear suddenly and startle her. She was in her bedroom either asleep or sitting in her chair and crocheting while she waited for me.

Rosa was from Mexico. She was the matriarch of this extended family that flowed in and out of her house, and she felt she should be treated with all the respect that her title deserved. However, her descendants were modern Hispanics with busy lives of their own and they gave her neither the attention nor the respect she needed.

Her grandson was a gang leader whose room was littered with "crime scene" police tape and sleeping or drugged friends. Usually, his wife hung out in the kitchen with their one-year-old son. Other young mothers with babies sat around the table talking, cooking, and eating. I never knew who they were or how they fit into the family. The most frequent argument I overheard was whose turn it was to buy groceries. An industrial-size pot of something (beans, soup, stew) cooked on the stove, but according to their conversations, there was never enough food. When her grandson awoke, he staggered half-dressed into the kitchen.

"What's there to eat?" he said. "Don't just sit there. Fix me a sandwich." He was routinely in trouble with the law. He bragged about the number of women he had sex with the night before or alluded to the crimes he successfully pulled off.

Rosa's daughter, Catrina, was occasionally at our sessions if she wasn't working. She was my best hope at translating because most of the others said they didn't speak Spanish, always right before they began chattering away in this foreign tongue. One day Catrina decided to unload some of her burdens and told me about the tragedies, violence, and deaths in the family, shaking her head "no" the entire time.

"You got kids?" she asked.

"No, I don't," I said. This was before I had a foster son.

"You smart," she said. "Don't never have no kids. I did all the right things. I took my son to church and taught him right from wrong. I don't know how he turned out to be in a gang. Just don't know what I did wrong. Don't never have no kids. You just don't know how they gonna turn out.

"And now this has gone and happened to Mama. And I got to work. She don't understand. I don't have no husband. She wants me to stay home and take care of her. I can't do that. I got me a good job. I can't be goin' and takin' no time off. I got to work."

Rosa stayed mainly in her bedroom as if these other people, some family and some not, had claimed the front of her house. Once a day, she walked to the front room and waited in her rocker for Meals on Wheels to deliver lunch. She carried it back to the kitchen to eat with whoever was there at the time, and then she shuffled back to her bedroom.

Besides the semiprivacy of her bedroom, there was one room in the house that she had claimed for her own. A small room off the kitchen appeared to have been a mudroom at one time, equipped with an outside door to the driveway. Now it was Rosa's sanctuary—the place where she prayed dutifully an hour every day. She decorated it with pictures of Christ, statues of Mary and Jesus, candles, Christmas lights, and rosaries. Since she no longer had the energy to leave the house, I imagined it to be her church—a sacred space she created in this house of chaos.

Rosa was eighty years old when I met her. She stood four feet and ten inches tall but hunched over so she appeared even shorter. Her Dutch-boy haircut made her look young. Her face was expressive, perhaps because that's who she was or maybe because she was compensating for the language difference. Her eyes were as questioning as a child's.

Rosa and I communicated through pantomime and a few isolated words. She had sprained her wrist two months before my first visit. It hurt all the time, but especially when she crocheted. The doctor told her there was nothing he could do for it, and there really wasn't anything medically to do except wait. However, Rosa hurt. In her mind, no one was paying attention to her pain or trying to help her. I massaged some analgesic cream into her hand and wrist. I knew it might not help, but it wasn't going to hurt anything to try. I bought an elastic splint at the drugstore so she could stabilize her wrist when she crocheted. It also served as a reminder not to use her wrist when she didn't have to.

As she began to trust me more, I included massage of her shoulders and upper back to help her relax from her continual pain and stress. She complained less of pain over time, but I'll never know if it was actually anything physical I did, or simply that I provided her with the emotional support and attention she needed to deal with it.

I introduced Rosa to activities she might enjoy other than crochet. She painted a birdhouse using small, careful strokes. I discovered her sanctuary at this time because she asked me to put her project in it to dry. Painting required that she sit at the kitchen table, and since the flow of people made her nervous, she went back to crocheting so she could stay in her bedroom.

Not long before I met her, Rosa had had other creative interests. Her home health aide, who worked for her for about a year before I got a referral, told me that one day Rosa had taken a few of her measurements. By the next visit, Rosa had completely finished a dress for her, which explained the abandoned sewing machine in the front room. The potted plants in the front yard had been placed there and arranged by Rosa. She asked her home health aide to water them, since it was hard for her to get up and down the uneven steps. Now her main creative outlet was crochet, and it was as important as eating and breathing for Rosa to continue to create.

One day, Catrina showed me some of Rosa's needlework. "Mama done this when she was only nine years old," she said. "Can you believe that? It looks like a grown person's work."

The embroidery piece was a five-inch square of the Madonna holding the baby Jesus, with astonishing detail of tiny stitches and vibrant colors.

Catrina began pulling crocheted pieces out of a cardboard box. "Look at all this," she said. "You can't find work like this no more. She's got dress collars, doilies, dresser scarves. Just look at these curtains. Here's two matching pillowcases."

I took each piece, one at a time, and laid it out on the dark bed-spread so I could see the designs.

"She's got anything you'd want," Catrina said. "Parrots, geese, angels. Look at these horses. You like horses, don't you? She made all these up in her head by looking at pictures in books. She never learned to read no English."

"Rosa, this is incredible," I said. "Catrina, thanks so much for pulling all these out. I had no idea Rosa was such an artist."

"They're all for sale, if you know anybody who wants to buy these," she said. "Tell them other nurses, too. Mama needs the money. She wants to sell them." Catrina and Rosa talked in Spanish while I continued looking at each piece.

A couple of weeks later, I decided that I wanted to buy one of the horse designs. I was sure that I was doing Rosa a favor by buying her work and I wanted it as a special gift for a friend. I knew that you were never supposed to use family members to translate, because they tended to interpret, then translate. But Catrina was my only choice, so I told her what I wanted. They argued back and forth for a while and finally Catrina told me that her mother had decided not to sell any of the pieces. I said that I understood. I tried to divert their attention when they began arguing again. "She says she'll sell you the piece for ten dollars," Catrina said. I handed Rosa twenty-five, hoped it was enough, and learned my lesson. It was not worth the anxiety I felt not being able to communicate directly.

Rosa's house was stacked from floor to ceiling with boxes full of things that no one used, but no one wanted to throw away. Roaches and mice lived among all this clutter so Rosa got a kitten to help with the pest control. The kitten was quite mischievous and spent most of her time teasing Isla, Catrina's Pomeranian, rather than chasing mice. But she earned her keep by entertaining Rosa. The only times I heard Rosa laugh was when the dog and kitten became a ball of fur tumbling through the room, unable to get their footing on the slick linoleum floor.

Rosa added her own touch to the drama in the house when it got to be too much for her to handle. She periodically threatened to sell the house and move into a nursing home so she could get better care than her family was willing (or able) to give her. She had a real estate agent appraise the house so everyone took her seriously. Then they tried a little harder and she dropped the threat. She used this tactic to control her family in the only way she knew how. Because Rosa's family was such a constant stress to her, the social worker told me that I should be glad I couldn't speak Spanish, but I never was. I would have loved to be able to talk with her and let her unload some of her burden.

Rosa's health declined with all the added stress. She began having abdominal pain so I added more time to my massage. Instead of sitting, she lay on the bed so I could include her legs and feet. She began to relax deeply enough to fall asleep.

One of the last things I did for her was make a communication board. She couldn't speak English and her tracheotomy made it difficult for her to speak at all. She had adapted well to pantomime, but as she got worse, I knew she would have less energy to communicate. I made a simple board with pictures and English and Spanish words to communicate basic needs.

One day as I was leaving, Rosa walked outside and picked out an ivy to give me. This may not seem like a big task for most people but it was very difficult for her to get up and down the steps and bend over to select just the right plant. It sits in my living room today and I think of her every time I water it. The simple gift is so important.

Despite the poverty, stress, and constant chaos, Rosa was able to maintain a sanctuary to feed her spiritual needs and continue her art in order to surround herself with beauty. I often saw her sit in the chair next to her bed, manipulating the crochet thread with the mindfulness of saying the rosary. Despite the language and cultural differences, we were able to connect through mutual respect, acceptance, and love.

I now vaguely remember the anxiety I had about our language barrier those first few weeks. I remember her pointing to her wrist and scrunching up her face in pain. I placed her hand on a pillow in her lap and gently began massaging it with analgesic cream. Gradually, I used deeper massage, carefully watching her face for any sign of increased pain. I tensed my shoulders and then exaggeratedly relaxed them, and then massaged her shoulders to remind her to relax, too. I spoke to her in English, hoping she would be able to pick up a few words, or understand the inflections in my voice.

I don't know how much I helped her physically. But I know that as I ended each session those last few weeks by placing a kiss on her cheek and telling her that I loved her, she looked deeply into my eyes and answered the same. She really just wanted the simplest thing—love and attention at the end of her life.

The poor need not only bread.
The poor also need beauty.

~ MONSIGNOR HILDEBRAND

"We Don't Need Any More Birdhouses"

Tom

Tom fought pulmonary fibrosis and cancer for a decade. Now his six-foot, two-inch frame looked like a skeleton. His tooled Western belt was fastened at the last hole to cinch his baggy pants. His name, which should have been centered in the back, was now over to the left. His thin chest and arms hid underneath a long-sleeve, baggy cotton shirt. He leaned to one side or the other so he could hold on to furniture while he walked. He carried the tension of his constant pain in his jaw and forehead.

I first met with Tom and his wife, Irene, on a Friday. We sat stiffly in the living room. I came to evaluate Tom for therapy. Instead, Tom and his wife evaluated me.

"I want to be able to work in my shop," Tom said. "I made almost every piece of furniture you see in this house. I made that coffee table."

"Wow, you're really good," I said.

"Used to be," he said. "Can't lift more than ten pounds now—doctor's orders. And the thing is, I get tired real fast. I'm always hooked up to this oxygen." He rubbed above his left ear and then adjusted the tubing.

Irene sat with her arms folded over her ample stomach. She leaned back in her chair so she could look down at me, scrutinizing everything

I said. "He's got too much time on his hands and it makes him a nervous wreck. He wants you to figure out how he can go back to work."

"The nurse said you could help me," he said.

"Well, the first thing would be to talk about adapting what you do," I said. "Have you ever considered making smaller projects that don't weigh as much or take as much time?"

Irene threw her arms up in the air. "No, no, no. We don't need any more birdhouses."

"No, I couldn't do that," he said. "I'm used to building furniture. I just couldn't go back to building birdhouses. It's too demeaning."

"OK, is there anyone you want to make a gift for? Maybe that will give us an idea."

"No, I've already made everyone a piece of furniture. And now I couldn't make anything up to my standards."

"He never charged for a piece of furniture he made anyone," Irene told me. "Even if they asked him to make it. He never charged anyone a cent."

"Sounds like you're very generous," I said to Tom.

"Oh, you can't even imagine," Irene said. "If something needed fixing at church, Tom's the first person they called. He's also done stuff for the Little League, Boy Scouts, Lions Club—you just can't begin to imagine."

"So what do you think?" he asked. "Can you show me how to get back to work?"

"Could you possibly sit down while you do some of your work?" I asked.

"Well, I've got a chair—" he said.

"He can't sit down while he works," Irene said. "He gets tired while he sits, too. That chair hurts his back and it's real hard. You'll have to come up with something better than that."

"OK," I said. "Let's take a look at your shop. Maybe I'll get some ideas. Would you mind showing me the rest of the furniture you made before we go out?"

They showed me around the house while I complimented him on each piece of furniture. Irene showed me everything she made, too. He made the bed, but she made the bedspread, quilt, dust ruffle, pillow shams, and matching curtains. He made the corner shelf that held the hundred-year-old oil lamp, but it was Irene's design.

Out in the shop, I made a few suggestions. Pad the chair with pillows. Move a tall stool next to the workbench and table saw. Set up his second oxygen tank out here. With each suggestion I made, Tom opened his mouth to ask a question or make a comment but Irene interjected and told me why each of my ideas wouldn't work. We worked on this for about two hours that first day. I left feeling defeated, glad it was the weekend. On my way home, I tried to think of ways to help him, but knew Irene would sabotage each of my ideas. I had already made some of my best suggestions and was told they were no good.

On Monday, I called back to admit defeat. I rehearsed while the phone rang. "I'm sorry, but I don't think I'm going to be able to help you. I've already used all my best ideas."

Irene answered the phone. "I got some pillows and fixed his chair," she said. "When are you coming?"

"Uh, tomorrow? Around three?" I asked. "Does that work?"

"Make it three-thirty so he has time to wake up from his nap," she said. "Pull in the driveway and use the back door."

The den was twice the size of the living room. An eight-by-ten brown, oval braided rug sat in the middle of the room on beige linoleum. The couch was brown and beige plaid that dated back forty years. The Early American coffee and end tables were similar to the ones my parents had in the sixties. A covered glass bowl filled with individually wrapped peppermints sat next to the *Reader's Digest*s and *Texas Highways*. The TV sat at one end of the long room; their mom and pop La-Z-Boys faced it from the opposite end. Each of them had avocado green TV trays next to their chairs. Irene had a black rotary phone, TV remote control, the latest *TV Guide*, a box of Kleenex, and a stack of opened mail on her table. A spool of crochet thread attached to an unfinished project usually sat on top of her craft magazines and folded newspapers on the floor. A small wastebasket made out of rolled sheets from magazines was nearby. A box of Kleenex and a glass of water were on Tom's table. Childhood pictures of their grown son hung on the dark paneled walls. A wooden plaque hung near Irene's chair: "If mama ain't happy, ain't nobody happy."

I had a feeling the rest of the house was rarely used anymore. The bedroom that had been converted to Tom's office wasn't needed now. He no longer had to sit at his oversized desk where he used to write letters, pay bills, plan finances, and calculate his taxes: Everything was done. A few utility bills needed to be paid every month; Irene did that at the kitchen table.

An RV was parked in the driveway, also unused now. They loved to tell about road trips they'd taken with caravans of other retired couples. Once, when Tom was looking for a project he wanted to show me, I got to see the inside of the RV. It was a miniature version of their home—crafty, dated, clean, and organized.

The heart of the home for Tom was his workshop. This was his creative space where he had designed and built elaborate pieces of furniture and made simple household repairs. Like the house, it was clean and well organized. Walls were covered with hanging hand tools. Homemade shelves held rows of baby food jars filled with nails, screws, nuts, and bolts, and he could usually find what he wanted without hesitation. An old metal desk was used for planning and drawing; drawers were perfectly ordered with files of designs. A table saw sat in the middle of the bay for easy access. A band saw and jigsaw sat against the wall. The blue Park Avenue sedan in the other half of the two-car garage reminded me that this was a hobby, not a profession.

"What kinds of things do you do with other patients?" Tom asked.

"Well, some of them work on overcoming physical problems like exercising to keep up their strength. Some of them make gifts to say good-bye. Some of them need a hobby like crocheting or painting wooden projects."

"Really?" he said. "Where do you get the wooden projects? What do they look like?"

I went out to my car and brought a few in for him to see. "You paid seven dollars for that hat rack?" he said. "Shoot, I could make it with about a dollar's worth of materials. Can you buy some lumber?"

By my next visit, he had made three hat racks similar to the one I showed him. "I've about used up all my scrap lumber, but we had an idea. There's a cabinet shop at the exit where you get off the highway. Why don't you go tell them what we're trying to do? I bet they'll give you some scraps."

The owner of the cabinet shop agreed to let me go through the scrap bins every week before they emptied them into the dumpster. Each week I backed my car up to the loading dock. Sometimes, the men helped me pick out the best pieces and loaded them into my trunk. The size of the pieces determined what the projects would be.

Initially, Tom went out to the shop with his wife and me in tow. We awaited his instruction, ready to set up the machines or lift lumber. After the first few sessions, we usually stayed in the house and planned activities for him to do during the week.

"What do you need this week?" Tom asked.

"Well, let's see," I said. "I have all these one-inch slats. How about some boxes with two solid sides and two slatted sides?"

"No," Irene said. "Those slats would make perfect trivets. I've got an apple design that will make a perfect pad for a hot pan."

"OK," I said. "Sounds like a good idea. I bet women will love them."

Then Irene asked me what other designs I liked, rejected whatever ideas I came up with, and often presented finished projects at the next session as *her* ideas.

Irene worked on her own projects, too. She crocheted angels for the Christmas tree, painted some of the wooden projects to give as gifts, and sewed decorative vests.

"You could do this," she said. "You could teach this to your other patients."

Each week, she taught me steps for making her current craft project. She gave me most of the instructions, then withheld a little until the next session. If something was cooking on the stove, she insisted I write down the recipe.

I tried to understand what she was going through. She always had to be better at everything than either Tom or me. It was childish and frustrating. What I came to realize was that as his life came to an end, she didn't want their working partnership to end a moment before it had to. She needed attention, too. She needed to feel creative and be recognized for her contribution. She needed something to concentrate on as the hours crept by. I learned that when Irene did all the talking, it was her way of maintaining control and contributing to his care. As her husband opened up more to working with me, she needed to have control over me. I knew I would have never gotten in their door a second time without her approval.

Over the ten months I worked with Tom, he made over four hundred projects. He also made adaptive equipment when I had special needs for other patients. Other patients were inspired and grateful when given his projects for completion.

What did Tom teach me? You can adapt your work without embarrassment or lessening its value. When there is no money, you can still find ways to be charitable. You can affect others' lives through your work. You can maintain a sense of purpose and self-worth. You can still create, even if it means working only minutes a day.

I think he wanted to stay active and have a creative outlet to fight the depression and pain. Even though working in his shop made him face his limitations, he was able to overcome the pain and initial humiliation to focus on his abilities to contribute. He had always been charitable and this was a way for him to continue and to focus on something outside himself.

What did Irene teach me? When they set up a hospital bed in the den about a week before Tom died, I glimpsed Irene's frailty, and made sense of her displaced anger toward me. For them, the bed wasn't an added comfort, but a symbol of the end. I watched her lose control of the one thing she still had complete control over—her home.

Tom and Irene had always worked together. When he was no longer able to work, she wanted my help. But she wanted it for herself. She wanted me to help her help him. That's the way she set up each session so that's what I did. I felt frustrated working under her control and criticism, but I knew it was the only way I could help him meet his goals. ℘

Do what you can, with what you have,
where you are.

∼ THEODORE ROOSEVELT

$\mathcal{S}$itting Vigil

Jennifer

Jennifer showed me one of her unfinished pointillism art projects consisting of tiny, intricate patterns, requiring precise skill and a steady hand. "I've got all these projects started," she said. "I just want to finish them." She held up a half-finished painting of some pool balls in a rack. "I *promised* my uncle I'd finish his; I was making it for his new poolroom. He's been waiting on it since before I got sick. I feel awful that it's not finished."

Jennifer was uncomfortable in her twenty-eight-year-old body. She was tense and weak, depressed and anxious. Her dark hair was short from recent chemo and her dark eyes looked tired from pain. An IV was attached to her left hand so there was restrictive, cautious movement. Once, I saw her walk with the help of her home health aide. She walked on tiptoes and her legs looked like they were asleep and tingling every time they touched the floor, then jerked away.

This was a newlyweds' apartment. Tall stacks of cardboard boxes filled most of the small living room. A few boxes were grouped around the tan love seat to provide extra seating. A bold black marker indicated the contents of each box—kitchen utensils, bathroom stuff, art supplies, unfinished projects. The kitchen was barely functional. A few plastic dishes were scattered here and there for reheating take-out in the microwave. Cleaning supplies sat on the kitchen counter for quick use when the mess got out of hand. They were never put away. Nobody knew where "away" was.

Three framed wedding pictures hung on the white wall in the opening between stacks of boxes. Now, boxes of medical supplies intermingled with their personal belongings. IV bags lay stacked with skeins of richly colored yarn. Such an odd combination seemed perfectly natural after a few visits.

The women in Jennifer's family sat huddled in the living room on the love seat, boxes, or floor as they crocheted. It was a quiet activity they could do while Jennifer slept. Crochet needles flew as they told stories, processed and reprocessed doctor's reports, grieved, prayed, and hoped. They added warmth and hominess to the clutter and disarray. Jennifer was living the last weeks of her life in the next room while her mother and aunts kept a close vigil. The last two weeks of her life, the men quit working and sat vigil, too.

It seemed more like migrant workers had set up camp in this apartment and soon they'd be moving on. I found that I wanted to unpack and give everything a home, but there was no desk for papers, no chest for clothes. In all the hours that her family was there, no one tried to turn this clutter into a home. I don't know whether they feared imposing on the new couple, if they were trying to be quiet while Jennifer slept, or if it was too sad to unpack because of the impermanence of the situation.

The sign on the bedroom door proclaimed, "Enter only with thoughts of unconditional love." The single hospital bed stood in the middle of the room for easy access, with IVs and monitors attached to Jennifer. A folding lawn chair sat next to the bed for Jennifer's visitors. It later occurred to me that Chuck, her husband, slept on the floor next to her bed at night.

Although her bedroom was makeshift, I was glad that someone had personalized it with a few of Jennifer's paintings, a quilt piece, needlework, and spiritual sayings. She loved art, after all, and needed beauty to help her transcend her reality. Get well cards overflowed a bulletin board, and vases of flowers (some wilted) sat on every available surface. It was an unsettling space to be in. As chaotic as it was, this room was her entire world now and she needed it to be safe and nurturing.

Since she wanted to try to complete her unfinished projects, I supported her, but I couldn't imagine her weak hands performing this kind of work. She, of course, was completely overwhelmed. A week passed and nothing happened.

At our next session, I encouraged her to try a less demanding project. She still wanted to try her painting so I supported her. Another week went by and no progress was made.

"Just to get your hands used to working again, how about making one of my projects?" I said. "I know you've got all these others started but you can pick something that won't take too long." Then, unknowingly, I asked the key question. "Is there anyone you'd like to make a gift for?" She painted a recipe box for her mother-in-law. She completed the project in two sessions and had a beautiful, handmade gift.

She initiated the next project. Her husband was turning thirty soon. "My plan is to give him thirty gifts," she said. "I suppose I could make some of them. Do you have a larger box—something he can put his car keys and change in?" The next week she told me she had put together a puzzle with her mom, something she hadn't had the patience for before now.

At one session when she was having a lot of pain, I suggested she try biofeedback. I had noticed a high school letter pinned to her bulletin board that she said she'd gotten playing varsity volleyball. Knowing she'd been athletic, I approached pain management from a standpoint of gaining control over her body, rather than the pleasure that comes from deep relaxation. She was in the vicious cycle of having pain, tensing her muscles in a protective response, and having more pain due to the increased tension.

We alternated between relaxation activities and making gifts, depending on how she felt when I arrived. I left relaxation tapes for her to listen to when she needed them.

At my last session, Jennifer's aunt greeted me at the door.

"Oh dear," she said. "I'm sorry no one called. I'm afraid you've wasted a trip. Jennifer has slipped into a light coma."

"That's OK," I said. "Since I'm already here, would you mind if I stay? I'd like to finish her project for her."

The living room was full of people. I waved, said "hello," and made my way to the bedroom. As I left the room, I heard the aunt who met me at the door explain who I was to the newcomers.

Jennifer's breathing was heavy and labored. Her mother and cousin sat on the floor, taking their turns with her for a two-hour shift. I turned to her mother. "Do you mind if I stay for a while?"

She nodded. "Go ahead. Take your time."

I picked up Jennifer's hand. "Jennifer, I want to put the second coat of varnish on the hat rack for your husband since you're not feeling well today." I pulled out the project, set up supplies, and began working.

"There must be ten people in the living room. You sure have a lot of people that care about you. Are they all family?" I asked Jennifer but looked over to her mother for an answer.

"Mostly," she said. "Her aunt and uncle are here from Dallas for a few days. Two of her high school friends stopped by earlier."

"Who brought the flowers? They're beautiful. I love irises and roses together," I asked Jennifer but again looked to her mother for an answer.

I continued talking to Jennifer, involving her mother and cousin while I painted. It took about ten minutes to complete. I wiped Jennifer's forehead with a wet washcloth. "Jennifer, are you able to open your eyes for a minute and look at this? It really turned out well. I like the color you picked. Chuck's going to love this."

She opened her eyes for about five seconds. I held the hat rack up for her but I could see she was having difficulty focusing. "I'll put it under your bed to dry. Your mother knows where it is. She'll make sure Chuck gets it, if you're not able to give it to him."

I placed it under the bed and went into the bathroom to wash the brush. When I came back to put the supplies away, I asked her mother, "Do you mind if I say good-bye?"

"No. Do whatever you want." She was more relaxed now. I wanted closure. I also wanted to show them how to say good-bye in case they hadn't been able, but I didn't want to do anything that would cause them anxiety if they weren't ready to hear it. It is, after all, a private act and I could have done it silently in meditation.

"Jennifer, I have really enjoyed knowing you and working with you these past few months. I want to thank you for working so hard when I knew you didn't feel like it. You've made many beautiful gifts. You know, they're much more than recipe boxes or art projects—they're gifts of immeasurable love. I can tell by all the cards, flowers, phone calls that interrupted therapy, and this apartment full of people that you are dearly loved. Someone will always be here with you. When it is time I hope you have an easy transition."

Jennifer needed me to support her to continue with her own art before she would trust me enough to try something new. She needed a goal, a focus outside herself. I broke a short-term activity down into manageable steps so she wasn't overwhelmed by all the projects that needed to be finished. I also involved her in an activity that met her aesthetic needs, while providing fast results. The combination of these steps got her over the hump of paralyzing depression into activity.

She never finished her own art projects. She was too weak to work with fine detail. Instead, she left behind some thoughtful, simple gifts that will be treasured.

The quality of mercy is not strain'd.
It droppeth as the gentle rain from heaven
upon the place beneath: It is twice blessed;
It blesseth him that gives, and him that takes.

~ WILLIAM SHAKESPEARE,
The Merchant of Venice

ℬringing New Meaning to Life

Donald

"If I quit eating and drinking, my doctor said it will take a few days to die," Donald said. "I'll slip into a coma. She promised to make sure I'm comfortable. No heroic measures."

We had talked about his choices before. Always clinically—never emotionally. He wanted to die peacefully and on his own terms. I couldn't let him die without telling him how I felt. "You know, I'll respect whatever you choose. I might want to make the same choice someday. I won't know that till I get there. But I need to tell you how I feel. I wish you wouldn't. I'll miss you. I'll miss coming to see you. I'll miss our talks."

His face softened and he laughed. "Thanks. I appreciate you saying it. But it's OK. It's what I want. If I don't do this, I'll die of suffocation—an agonizing death. I'll choose a date and I'll know when the time is right. Right now, I'm thinking about March fifteenth."

"That's only six weeks away."

"I know. I want to start while I still feel good."

Donald was a slight man, weighing only about a hundred pounds. He was always cold in the nursing home so he wore a knitted hat, thick wool socks, and a light jacket over his pajamas. Sometimes he even wore gloves. He smiled and greeted his guests but quickly withdrew to his tense, collected state. He looked like someone who was in a constant state of "fight or flight"—all of his energy coiled, ready for an action that need never happen.

"When I decided to come into the nursing home, I gave away everything I owned except my clothes," he said. "The nursing home set up this card table so I can have a desk. Would you be able to bring me a few office supplies—pens, pencils, pencil holder, paper clips, desk organizer—things like that? Oh, and a small note pad—small enough to fit in my pocket." Most of this I brought from home. It was a simple request, yet important to a former college professor.

Donald had taught art history, French, and Spanish literature. "I've been working on an article for several months. Without going into too much detail, it's a critical analysis of some classical pieces of art. I don't know what my chances are of ever getting this article published. It's quite controversial. It won't make me popular. But at least I want to finish it."

Donald had a routine in the nursing home. He slept much of the day because he was tired from lack of oxygen. He ate at scheduled mealtimes, saw hospice visitors, wrote his article, did his stretching exercises in bed, and argued with his roommate. "I hate my roommate. He's a disgusting, vicious man. He has no respect for anyone."

"Have you asked to be moved?" I asked him.

"They won't," he said. "There aren't very many men here and they said no one else wants to move. Most of the men here are out of their minds. Why can't they just put me in a room with someone who sleeps all day? That would be fine with me. The women here are awful. At lunch, I try to make polite conversation but most of them won't even talk to me. They're bitter old ladies."

One afternoon when I was visiting, they served supper early. "Under that metal lid is a grilled cheese sandwich that's inedible," he said. He removed the cover from his plate and lifted an edge of the sandwich. The bottom piece of bread was soggy and half of it stuck to the plate when he lifted it out. "You'd think they could get this right. How hard is it to make a grilled cheese sandwich?"

"Yuck, the whole thing's soggy. Doesn't look very good," I said. "Have you asked them to try a paper towel under it or could they bring it to you uncovered?"

"I've done all that, but every evening I get the same thing," he said. "They don't care. I get the same breakfast, lunch, and supper every day. They have no idea how to feed a vegetarian—said I'm the only one they ever had."

Donald lived in the same nursing home that Lana, another of my patients, had lived in a year earlier. "I've seen their food," I said. "It's never been very good. Can I bring you some snacks?"

Donald moved to a different nursing home within the month. It was the one Maude had lived in—beige rooms, exposed pipes, linoleum floors. He had his own room at the end of the hall and it was quiet, the way he liked it. He was able to control the temperature, so he quit wearing his hat and coat. He looked much more relaxed. People respected his privacy and knocked before they came into his room.

I helped him make a list of foods he liked that were easy to prepare and suggested he make an appointment with the dietitian.

"How'd it go?" I asked.

"Good, she had some ideas, too," he said. "We came up with five different meal plans—some modified from their regular menus and some items she's getting just for me. No more grilled cheese. Very nice lady. We'll see if she does what she says."

"Well, sounds like a good start," I said. "At least she listened."

"I brought a stack of calendars. I thought you might enjoy looking at these," I said. "There's a little bit of everything, but some of them are art. If you like any of the pictures, I'll help you put them up around your room."

I never really thought he would use them for decoration since he seemed to prefer a life of minimalism. At most, I hoped it would give us something to talk about. When I came back a week later, about two hundred pictures had been carefully arranged on the walls.

"What do you think?" he asked.

"What happened to your dull, beige walls?" I asked. "This is great! It's like being in an art gallery." Abstract designs intermingled with photographs of thousand-year-old pottery. Wild animals sat next to landscapes of deserts, forests, and marshlands.

He carefully selected his favorite pictures and placed them on the walls according to color, content, shape, and size. He studied them tirelessly from his bed and discussed them with everyone that visited. "How do you think they got that picture of the polar bear? Where was the photographer? Do you think he's actually looking into the camera or was it taken at a great distance? Do you see that picture over there? That's called a fractal. It's a computer-generated design. How do you think they make that? Does the image remind you of anything?"

He got out the leftover calendars. "Maybe you could help me with the door," he said. "I need just the right pictures for coming and going. How about this peaceful landscape? What about this mandrill for the front of the door? He has the most brightly colored face on the planet." He had also taken a few pictures from the nursing home's magazine rack. After this, he became the volunteer caretaker of the magazine rack, keeping it orderly and well supplied.

He also became interested in the study of nature. We put up a bird feeder and he asked his social worker to take him to the bookstore for a book on birds. He listened for reports of deer in the area. He read articles in *National Geographic* before putting them on the rack for others.

At one of our last visits, Donald asked if there were any pictures I wanted. I chose a photograph of a Native American bowl. He also took down his two favorite pictures of fractals and said he wanted me to have them. He looked directly into my eyes. "These may be worth something, someday," he said.

The thought went through my mind that they were just mass-produced, torn-off pages from calendars. Donald was educated. He had to know this, too. But it occurred to me that he wanted to give me something of value. He didn't own anything of monetary value and he hadn't been interested in making any gifts. He gave me what he had—something that had astonished and entertained him from the minute he saw them. I thanked him graciously for his precious gifts.

He hadn't kept his first date of fasting on March fifteenth, or his second. But by June, he had to quit talking to catch his breath during our session. I said my good-byes and hoped he wouldn't keep this date, either. But during the week, I got a message that he had started his fast.

Donald created a world of new interests and meaning at the end of his life that he shared with all of us. When I met him, we didn't have much to talk about. I tried to help him get his needs met, but our conversations felt rigid, without an easy flow. At the end of his life, he had become an enthusiastic conversationalist. He invited people to see his room, and then asked philosophical questions that started lively discussions. He studied his new interest—nature. He said he was agnostic, but looked forward with great interest to finding out what happens after death.

He was interviewed for a newsletter a month before he died. The title of the article was "Bringing New Meaning to Life."

"Having hospice has made all the difference," he said. "There are easily five or six people who come out so I have company during the week. I have a tendency to forget that they're from hospice and to say that they're just my friends."

The greatest part of our happiness or misery
depends on our dispositions and not on
our circumstances.

~ MARTHA WASHINGTON

"$\mathcal{A}$ Good Man Is Hard to Find"

Peggy

Peggy and her husband shared a lifetime of celebration. Her husband had served as a military officer and later as an ambassador. They had traveled the world and entertained extensively.

"When I was just a girl, I studied piano, voice, and dance," Peggy said. "I loved to perform. I was a cheerleader in high school, if you can believe that, and I always wanted to be a cabaret singer. Rather risqué for a military wife so I ended up performing at officers' clubs and my own parties instead."

Peggy pointed to a photograph. "Look at this one. One of my life's dreams was to perform the Dance of the Fans. I studied classical Japanese dance for five years." A picture of a younger Peggy in a kimono, with the elaborate fans positioned in front of her, documented this.

Peggy loved to tell stories about the other pictures and artifacts from all over the world that decorated her modest retirement home. Favorite pictures of her family and friends hung on the walls with a robust, vibrant Peggy in all of them. The frail sixty-eight-year-old woman gazed at the pictures. "I always had trouble with my weight from all the rich party food," she said. Her weak hands lifted the walker as she laughed nervously, and carefully turned her ninety-five pound frame toward me. "Sure wish I had that problem now."

When they retired and moved back to the states from Japan, Peggy noticed that her husband was having a problem with alcohol. They led a quieter life now; the parties were over. Yet, her husband continued drinking daily. He denied there was a problem when she asked him to quit. She joined Al-Anon and once again had a big support system and social outlet. When Al-Anon had conferences or parties, she signed up to be on the entertainment committee, and still performed as often as possible. She enjoyed this lifestyle for nine years before becoming ill with a chronic lung disease. That's when she became a hospice patient.

When I met Peggy, she and her husband were seated in their recliners in front of a blaring TV. He made no effort to turn the volume down, so she yelled at me that she had arthritis pain and wanted a massage. I immediately suggested we find a quieter room where we could talk and not interrupt her husband's program. He showed no interest in what we were doing and seemed happy to be left alone.

She looked frail so I gently massaged her muscles and moved her joints through their full ranges of motion.

"You can go deeper, hon," she said. "I like a really deep massage."

"If you're not sore from this massage, next time I'll go deeper—I promise," I said. "I have to go slowly to make sure that I don't cause any damage."

At our next session, she reported that she felt fine after the last time and again she asked for a deeper massage. She requested that I work even deeper throughout the session. I soon realized that it wasn't arthritic pain she was primarily complaining about because the deeper massage would have been intolerable. She was complaining about muscular tension. I continued moving her joints through their full ranges of motion in order to keep her flexible, but I began giving deeper massages and teaching stress management techniques. She experimented with different techniques until she found a few that worked for her. Something that seemed to be important to her success was to set aside time every day and practice in the room where I massaged her. She asked her husband to turn the TV down and not let anyone disturb her for about an hour. If she tried to practice anywhere else in the house, she couldn't relax as deeply. This became her ritual. Even though she was using supplemental oxygen, she learned to make her breathing more even and steady. She visualized receiving a massage and letting go of muscle tension, one body part at a time. On days when she had less focus, she used a guided imagery tape. She also bought a pillow with an electronic neck massager but it was too jarring. I showed her how to position her neck and back with pillows and place a towel over the massaging knobs to diminish their pressure, and then she enjoyed using this. Most days she fell asleep while working on her stress management. Being awake without stress and pain was the goal, but if she fell asleep, that was fine. Some days she practiced for ten minutes, became frustrated, and quit until the next day. However, she practiced regularly and benefited from her efforts for a few months.

She opened and closed her hands. "This pain in my hands hurts all the time," she said. "I have trouble opening my pills."

"Well, that's no problem," I said. "We can ask the pharmacist to give you easy-open lids or ask the nurse to organize them in a schedule box for you. Have you thought about a hobby? Lots of people tell me that things like crochet help arthritic hands."

"No, I don't like anything like that," she said. "I've never been a hobby kind of person."

"What about playing the piano?" I asked.

"Oh, it's been years," she said. "I doubt I could play a single note anymore."

"I bet if you played just ten minutes a day it would really loosen up your joints and help your pain," I said.

She began practicing and eventually played songs for her visitors. Sometimes the songs were unrecognizable, but we all marveled at her ability to play in her weakened condition. The attention and praise seemed to be as therapeutic as the improvement in her hands.

During this time, she smiled more and had fewer complaints for her caregivers. She became more outgoing and focused less on her symptoms. One day while I massaged her, she told me about a statewide Al-Anon convention she had helped organize and that she had performed a song as part of the entertainment. When she sat up from the massage, she belted out all the verses of "A Good Man Is Hard to Find." This woman with poor lung capacity, who was always on supplemental oxygen, didn't miss a beat. I am continually amazed at the resiliency of people when they're being creative.

Another day, her Al-Anon friends, Marguerite and Thelma, showed up at the same time I did. She invited them to sit in the room with her while she got her massage.

"You know, this disease has really gotten to be too much," Peggy told us. "I'm ready to die and go to heaven."

"I've made a little progress on my relationship with my father," Marguerite said. "Alcoholism is a terrible thing. It robbed me of my childhood. You know how I was always afraid of my father. It's affected me all my life—every relationship I've ever had with men."

"Oh, I agree," Thelma said. "I don't know what I would have done without the support of Al-Anon."

"I'm in pain and it's getting worse all the time," Peggy said. "I've accepted that I'm going to die, and I'm ready."

"I'm going to the state convention this year," Marguerite said. "Are you going to be able to make it?"

"No, my husband's been too sick," Thelma said. "I better stay home and take care of him."

I wanted to scream at them: *Shut up and listen—your friend is dying and she's giving you the most intimate gift she has.* The next week when I saw Peggy, she laughed when I told her my reaction. She had just shrugged it off, happy to have the company.

The community newspaper ran a feature article about Peggy being a hospice patient. With the help of her volunteer, she made copies of the article and sent it, instead of Christmas cards, to friends. The article explained to everyone why they hadn't heard from her, since this was out of character for such an extrovert. Soon she began receiving cards from all over the world.

One day while I was with her, she got an audiotape from Japan. It was from a blind man whom she had helped get an audition for a job playing piano. We listened to it while she got her massage. In his broken English, he told her that he had heard about the article from a mutual friend and in response, he had made this tape of her favorite songs. He spoke between songs about what her friendship had meant to him and how it had continued to help him throughout his life. It was a simple and tremendously powerful gift. She laughed and cried throughout the session. She had me turn off the tape player when she remembered a story she needed to tell. She added this tape to her relaxation ritual so she could hear it over and over.

Most of Peggy's fear was about living, not dying. Because her husband drank, he wasn't able to care for her adequately. In fact, she often had to take care of him. She politely, but sometimes tearfully told us, "No, I don't think he's drinking." We all knew he was, but we tried to respect her privacy until we felt it was threatening to her health. Finally, we intervened at a family conference. Her nurse, social worker, chaplain, volunteer, nurse's aide, and I gathered in Peggy's bedroom with her and her husband. Her nurse, Lori, started the meeting. "Peggy has had more pain lately. We've increased her medication but it seems she's missed a few doses. Can you help remind her to take her medication?" she asked Bill, Peggy's husband.

"Sure," he said. "I didn't know there was a problem."

"Can you also keep a medication log so we can see what time of day she has the most pain?" Lori asked. "That way, we'll know when to adjust her pain pills."

"Listen, I don't know what you people are doing here," he blurted. "We're doing fine. There aren't any problems."

"Well, actually, Bill, there are problems. Peggy's losing weight. She's getting weaker. She's requiring more sleep and more medication. She's not eating regular meals, and she's still trying to take care of the house, but she's not able. It's not safe to leave her alone in the house for more than an hour at a time. And lately, she's having anxiety attacks." She turned to Peggy. "Peggy, is this an accurate picture?"

Peggy nodded and lifted her shaking hand to wipe a tear away.

"Peggy, one alternative would be to go to a nursing home," Lori said. "I know you haven't wanted to in the past, but how do you feel about it now?"

"Absolutely not," Peggy said. She began crying. "I don't want to go. I want to stay here."

"Well, another solution would be to get more help in your home," Lori said. "Bill, do you think you could hire a part-time housekeeper?"

It occurred to me then that not taking better care of Peggy was part of his denial that she was going to die. It allowed him to pretend that she could still take care of herself. He agreed to follow some guidelines such as preparing her meals, helping her with medication and keeping a medication log, getting a part-time housekeeper, not leaving her alone in the house for more than an hour at a time, and not smoking in the same room where she was using oxygen. Two volunteers were assigned to her so her husband could get out of the house a little more. He was encouraged to visit with friends to help relieve his stress. If he stayed in denial, he had no support system.

Peggy's husband was a little more responsible for a short while. Then he was ticketed for a DWI and had to enter an alcohol day treatment program for six weeks. The housekeeper and volunteers filled in. Peggy worried about her husband and her uncertain future, and her stress increased. As soon as her husband was out of treatment, he began drinking again and Peggy finally gave up.

"I feel like I'll never smile again," she said. I tried to provide the safety for whatever she needed to do. I tried to not have expectations that I could fix things. I wanted to be open to whatever was happening with her during the time that I was with her. "This is too much to bear. I don't understand why I can't just go ahead and die."

She deteriorated rapidly. Her husband continued drinking and sleeping in his easy chair while the TV blared eighteen hours a day. Peggy had been asked earlier if she wanted to be moved to the hospital when she got closer to death. She refused, wanting to stay in the familiarity and privacy of her home. Her volunteers took turns staying with her and tried to provide emotional support for her husband as she went through the final stages of dying.

A month after Peggy's death, her husband moved closer to their son's family.

What did Peggy teach me? A person's need is often different from what it appears. Peggy asked for help with her arthritis. Movement and range-of-motion exercises are the treatment for arthritis. But Peggy wanted to be massaged, and she didn't want to admit she had stress. I also think she had another need for wanting massage. I think she was craving touch. During one of my visits, her husband was having neck pain and she asked if I could recommend anything for him other than massage because he didn't like to be touched. This was a clue that she might not be getting touch, which is essential to us all. She felt she couldn't say, "My husband is an alcoholic. I'm dying and I feel tremendous stress. No one ever touches me. Will you please just massage me?" It was much easier to blame the arthritis.

She needed me not to have any expectations. She began to trust that I wasn't going to make assumptions. If she smiled, I wouldn't require her to say she felt better. Or if she complained of pain, I wouldn't expect this to be a pattern. I tried to be open to whatever was happening with her. She responded by giving me the gift of allowing me to be with her through all kinds of emotions: fear, anger, laughter, singing, hurt, love, and finally—resignation.

I also learned that you're never so removed that you can't help if you want to. A man from another world, culture, and language touched her heart with an intimacy that her seemingly close friends would never have understood. It's easy to find every excuse in the world not to make contact with someone who is dying because it's awkward—I've done it, too. He so eloquently and simply said, "Your friendship has meant a lot to me and here's some songs that I remember you like." 🙢

Listening is a form of accepting.

∼ STELLA TERRILL MANN

"Why Didn't He Tell Me He Had AIDS?"

Gary

Gary was a breach baby, the last born in a family of ten. Despite the difficult delivery, the next day his mother took him with her to do the grocery shopping and laundry. Of all her children, she had always been closest to Gary. Even as a teenager, he had been the most sensitive and loving of her children. Perhaps Gary filled in emotionally for his father, who died of a brain tumor when Gary was only seven years old.

They lived in a remote area of North Carolina. Gary's mother never went to school nor learned to read. She worked in a poultry factory, skinning chickens while standing in icy water. She also had a variety of smaller jobs to help feed and clothe her family. "I was just proud to be able to take care of my family," she said. Gary embraced her values of honesty and hard work.

Her husband's name was tattooed on her left shoulder and her name had been tattooed on his, a declaration of their commitment to each other. "Oh, it was just some crazy thing we done one night after we first got married," she said in her soft, romantic drawl. But she thoughtfully rubbed her hand over it as she displayed it with pride, this representation of her life as a wife, a respected place in society. During that moment, it didn't seem like a crazy whim, but a deliberate declaration of love and permanence. Commitment was a value Gary learned from her, too. He was a dedicated partner to Frank till death.

These humble beginnings had their impact on Gary. He felt misunderstood because no one realized how he had grown up—where he had come from. He was obsessed with how others perceived him—"queer, fat, stupid, hick." He was often openly defensive about his disease.

"What's the matter?" he said. "You afraid of getting AIDS?"

I turned down the canned Coke he was handing me. "No, I'm allergic to corn syrup. See, look right here at the ingredients. Corn syrup. Thanks anyway."

At the age of seventeen, Gary moved to California, to live with a lover twice his age. Gary knew Frank took medication for a heart condition, but he was too naive and trusting to suspect other problems. It wasn't until Gary was in the last stages of AIDS that he realized he was taking the same medication as Frank. He grieved for Frank, knowing that he would never have another lover in this lifetime. His loss was an issue of conflicting emotions: love, deception, yearning, and grief. He stayed in a state of confusion because it seemed too much to process. When he was depressed, he asked the same questions over and over. "How could he have lied to me?" he asked. "Why didn't he tell me he had AIDS?" No wonder he couldn't trust any of us. The person he had loved most had betrayed him with his life.

Now Gary was in Texas. He was thirty and had AIDS, and a brain tumor like his dad. I met him two months earlier when I helped a friend with an art class for persons with AIDS. Gary lived alone and had become reclusive. He looked apprehensive as he extended his handshake to others. "Please don't hug me," he said. "I have to be careful about germs." He had a little trouble getting started, but soon enough became involved in a project. He attended sporadically and we always let him know how much we liked him being in class, because we knew how difficult it was for him to come.

Gary became hospitalized for a while after those initial meetings. His mother still lived in North Carolina and the rest of his family was estranged—afraid they would catch the virus. Gary had no one. A family of volunteers from the art class—Joe and Janice and their daughters, April and Karen—"adopted" Gary and became his primary caregivers. They visited him in the hospital and helped him get resettled in his apartment afterward. They brought food to him and invited him over for meals. They took him to movies or just hung out. They were warm and easygoing, and genuinely cared about him.

After the hospitalization, Gary became a hospice patient. Then he became my patient. When I arrived that first day, he seemed happy to see a familiar face. He showed me around his sparsely furnished apartment. Nothing about it told me who Gary was, except that he didn't have a lot of money: thinning shag carpet and dark paneled walls, motel windows with outdated, rubber-backed drapes, and stained linoleum in the sterile white bathroom and tiny kitchen. The couch was made of wooden slats with square, orange cushions, and a chair to match. A metal bookshelf in the living room had nothing on it. Twin beds and an almost empty dresser that seemed a little too shiny to really be wood stood starkly in the bedroom.

Gary told me that he was looking forward to a visit from his mother. I asked if he wanted to make a Mother's Day gift for her, since it was already the beginning of May. He jumped at the chance and followed me down the stairs to rummage through the projects I kept in the trunk of my car. He chose a wooden box shaped like a chicken that needed sanding and staining. He didn't want to work on it today, because he wanted to visit some more. He said he'd work on it on his own. I gave him directions for using the stain and showed him that they were written on the bottle. When I returned, he had finished the project but not followed the directions and it had taken days to dry, instead of minutes.

Our next visit was still a week before Mother's Day so he decided to make a gift for Janice, his volunteer mother. I asked him to work on it a little, while we visited. He was initially reluctant and the reason was soon apparent. He was having trouble positioning his body in relation to the project. Instead of just picking the project up in his hand and holding it at eye level so he could see small details, he distorted his body and bent over so he was eye level with the project on the table. I imagine this was the work of the tumor.

The day before Mother's Day, Gary met his mother at the bus station. She was tired and anxious from the long trip, but these feelings vanished when she spotted her son. Gary and his mother were inseparable the first three weeks of her visit. She became involved in his life again and actively participated in his hospice sessions with the nurse, social worker, chaplain, volunteer, and therapist. She told stories to give us insight into working with her son. She brought gifts for Gary to brighten up his apartment and mementos from his childhood that helped us know him better. Pictures of a younger, healthier Gary appeared on the walls. A small collection of ceramic dachshunds decorated the bookshelf. His mother even brought a patchwork quilt she made for his new apartment. One day I admired the fine detail on the crocheted doily on the kitchen table.

"Should we tell her the truth?" Gary asked. They looked at each other and laughed. "You know those strings you pull to open feed sacks?"

I looked at it more closely. "Wow! I would have never guessed." What they never knew was how much more beautiful it then became to me because of its transformation. Here was another gift Gary had gotten from his mother—the love of creating, making beautiful things.

One of Gary and his mom's favorite activities was to go to nearby apartment complexes where college students lived. They went through trash bins and brought home treasures that the "rich" kids had thrown away. This is how Gary got most of his clothes, and his apartment started looking "lived in." Throw pillows decorated the couch. A baby-blue princess phone was added to the bedside table. Bowling trophies appeared. Books began filling the empty shelves. A high-intensity lamp sat on

an end table. They brought home reams of unused paper and statio-
nery. Discarded art supplies were Gary's favorite. Cooking utensils and
a toaster oven worked in the kitchen. They carried home a set of canvas
and wood panels that they used as a room divider, so that each of them
could have more privacy in the bedroom. They found unused crepe
paper and party favors for the small birthday party Gary arranged for
his mother. What they didn't use, they gave away as gifts. Gary's mother
seemed to be having a wonderful time renewing her relationship with
him, and decided to stay indefinitely.

Gary had worked in construction since he was eighteen years old. He
knew how to work as part of a team for a common goal. The buildings he
helped create represented not only his time and hard work, but also part
of his love and soul. He enjoyed his work as his valued craft, his art. "I
feel like I'm going nuts in this apartment," he said. "I'm used to working."
His hospice volunteer suggested that he do some volunteer work at hospice. He came in for a couple of hours, two or three times a week, to help
with filing, mailing, and general office work. He got an engraved name
badge that made his job official, like all the paid workers. This helped
him for a couple of months, and after that he was too ill to continue.

He dreamed of being an artist, creating a place of escape. He told
me he wanted to understand perspective, depth of perception on paper.
Since it was too difficult to go to art class, he set up a small table next
to a window with his art supplies on display. He relived his construction
days through his art. He could no longer create buildings literally, but he
could create them on paper. He usually drew from pictures of buildings
collected from magazines. He added warm details of his own such as
plants, flowers, or the sun shining through a window.

Over the next couple of months, the severity of Gary's headaches
increased because of his tumor, and he spent his days smoking cigarettes and lying on the couch. His mood swings were unpredictable. On
a good day, he met me at the door and said, "Come on in here, darlin'.
Let's you and me get naked and make love all afternoon."

I played along. "Gary, I can't believe you said that in front of your mother. What's she going to think of me? Besides, you know I'm a married woman."

Other days he couldn't get off the couch to greet me. On those days, I reminded his mother to pull the shades for him, because any amount of glare intensified the pain.

His mother became anxious and depressed. Although some of this was about Gary's decline, a lot of it seemed to be because she was accustomed to living in the country and being outside—not in the city in a one-bedroom apartment, day in and day out. Hospice provided a volunteer to help Gary's mother cope with her stress. Once or twice a week, she had a lunch date and browsed through the nearby thrift stores to have some time for herself. She tended to come back full of renewed energy, relishing the attention and support she needed. "I'm just so proud we got to go to lunch," she said.

One day when I arrived, Gary was asleep so I sat and talked with his mother.

"He's always been such a good boy," she said. "Real sweet, that 'un. I'm 'fraid for him now. Why would anybody be a homosexual? It don't make no sense."

"I don't think it's a choice he made," I said. "It's just the way he is."

"I don't get it. I pretend, for his sake, it don't matter. I didn't raise him no different from my other sons. Now, God's punishing him with this disease. This ver-neer-ree-al disease." She wiped her tears.

"I don't believe Gary is being punished. Unfortunately, he got AIDS. People from all walks of life get AIDS: young and old, gay and straight, women and men—even babies. I don't think he's being punished."

"I can't never go back. I've been here too long. The rest of my family will do me like they done him. They'll be too 'fraid I'll give it to 'em. You think I have it yet?"

"No, ma'am. It's not like a cold or the flu. You can't get it from just being with someone who has it. You can only get it through an exchange of bodily fluids. But if you're worried, we can have you tested. That's something you don't need to be worrying about. I'll ask the nurse to go over universal procedures with you again—just to make sure you're doing everything safely."

She had been pretending to accept his lifestyle so convincingly that none of us suspected the pain she was in.

During his period of severe headaches, Gary got his days and nights mixed up. He woke up in the middle of the night and went to the living room to watch TV and smoke. He fell asleep while smoking and put a couple of cigarette burns in the carpet near the couch. I suggested a smoker's robot, which is a device that holds the cigarette in a stationary position over an ashtray while the person smokes through a flexible tube. He was intrigued by the novelty at first, but soon rejected it. We begged him to restrict his smoking unless someone was in the room with him, but he continued to smoke as he wanted. Gary got angry and defensive if his mother came out of the bedroom to "babysit" him, so she stayed in bed, paralyzed with fear of sleeping through a fire.

The three of us began a group project—a braided rug to go in front of the couch to protect the carpet from further ruin. I wanted to give them a project that they could do together, without a lot of set-up time. Gary was motivated at first, selecting colors and designing the shape and size. He soon realized that his mother would finish it for him, so he let her.

His body and mind went through too many changes in too little time. The cortisone caused his body to swell. His abdomen became distended and he no longer had clothes he felt comfortable wearing. As he got more lethargic and lost muscle tone, he also got clumsy.

He became demanding and abusive, so his mother went back to North Carolina. After she left, Gary felt guilty. In his semi-confused state, he got on a bus and followed her home. When his mother called to let us know where he was, we transferred his care to a local hospice and I didn't see him after that.

A week or so later, he decided that he had made a terrible mistake, and he came back to Austin. His adoptive family picked him up at the bus station and took him to the hospital, because he was now quite sick. In the hospital, he was agitated, unreasonable, and sometimes uncontrollable. He ripped IVs out and tried to go home, although he didn't have the energy to get out of bed. His adoptive family stayed with him through all of this, providing him with the unconditional love his mother had tried so hard to give him at the end of his life.

Gary was obsessed with others' negative perceptions of him. He craved companionship but was extremely uncomfortable—almost paranoid—in social situations. He wanted to fit in, but in his mind, he never did.

Gary's mother loved him so much that she was willing to risk her life (at least, in her limited knowledge of the disease) in order to take care of him. Although she had harsh judgments about his lifestyle, she was able to set them aside and take care of her dying son.

What I saw in Gary were values he learned from his mother. He was an honest and hard worker. When he was no longer able to work in construction, he became serious about creating buildings through art. He even volunteered at hospice, just to be working and productive. He was a dedicated partner and took care of his companion till death. He practiced generosity and made gifts for his mother and volunteer. When he had no money, he became creative and gathered a wealth of treasures. ✤

Call it a clan, call it a network, call it a tribe,
call it a family. Whatever you call it,
whoever you are, you need one.

~ JANE HOWARD

Bereavement

I hold these relationships as intimate and precious. Each person I worked with taught me to have a richer, deeper, fuller life. I consider it a privilege to have known each of these patients and shared this time with them.

I want to thank you for reading this far and for inviting these people into your life. This is just the tip of what you're about to learn when you work with your patient, friend, or family member. I honor your courage to continue and I honor it in any form that it takes for you.

At the hospice where I worked, the director of volunteers holds an annual luncheon to honor all of the volunteers. She refuses to single anyone out or have a "volunteer of the year" award. She knows that each person's contribution cannot be measured against another's. One person volunteers an hour a week filing paperwork in the hospice office. Another sits with a dying patient so the family members can get some sleep. Perhaps it is best stated by Martin Luther King Jr.: "Everyone has the power for greatness, not for fame but greatness, because greatness is determined by service."

I hope these stories have shown that by being with someone who is dying you can open to intimacy with yourself, another person, the world, life, and death. Achieving this level of intimacy simply requires that you open your heart. That's all. You don't need to have special skills or be able to figure out complex solutions to problems. You need to simply be willing to be with someone and listen to what his heart is saying.

Opening your heart to dying means accepting a fullness that you won't know otherwise. Small things will bring you richer pleasure, but the pain may be deeper, too. If you take only one lesson from these stories, I hope that it is the courage to try. Try on faith to let someone else open up to you. Trust that whatever your responses are, they're what the person needs because they're from your heart. In learning about the person you are with, you will learn immeasurably about yourself. Try a couple of visits, just to see what it's like. Don't be surprised if you begin looking forward to them. Don't be afraid to try; you can always do more than you think.

If you're working with a friend or family member, this may be a chance at deepening your relationship. If there's something you need or want from this person, rather than asking them to give it, open yourself more deeply to receiving. The best gifts often appear casually and unexpectedly.

A friend of mine who was dying told me that one of the hardest things she had to deal with was taking care of her friends' and family's emotional needs. She said that it was enough of a burden to wrestle with her own grief, loss, and pain. She was a minister and it was not only her role in life, but also her nature to give.

A few months before she died she asked me what it was like, having worked at hospice and now being with her through her experience. I thought about it and answered as honestly as I could. "Right now I'm not feeling grief. I'm just glad to get to spend some time with you and help out. I don't know how it will be when you get closer to death. All I know is that whatever it is, the choice I've already made is to be here with you."

It has been my experience that the more I have been able to open my heart to someone, the more I felt I was able to unburden them. This seems to be totally independent of whether I did something recognizable to the rest of the world, or not. Whether I worked with them for a year to create a legacy for their children or simply sat next to their bed, feeling helpless as they squeezed my hand while crying in pain, I can feel some ease knowing that I stayed with them. My pain is less if I've faced my own fears.

Being with someone you don't know until after diagnosis is much different than being with someone you've known before diagnosis. I'm frequently asked how I could work with hospice patients. "How do you deal with the sadness?" But it's easier than you might think. Most of us who knew someone who died, knew them also when they were healthy.

To learn that someone you know has a terminal prognosis or died unexpectedly is a shock to our systems. It requires a huge shift in our perception. It may require that we confront our own death. We may even begin grieving the loss as soon as we hear the diagnosis, long before their death.

If the person who dies is your friend or family member, you may feel devastated. I encourage you to journal, attend a support group, or find a bereavement counselor if you feel your grief is complicated. Create your own personal rituals for grieving.

The work of grief is to integrate the person who is no longer physically here into your heart. You may find that you are initially very tired, because grieving is hard work, and you are doing it twenty-four hours a day whether you are conscious of it or not. Your emotions may overwhelm you when you least expect it. You'll probably feel more vulnerable, like your nerve endings are exposed.

Many of your feelings may not even make sense to you. It's important to let yourself feel whatever you feel without judgment. Your grieving will probably last longer than you expect. Our society has a "get over it" attitude so you can be productive again. But in reality, grief is an ongoing process. As my friend Marion says, "Treat yourself like you would treat your best friend if this loss had happened to her."

But when I meet someone for the first time and I know that he is going to die, I don't experience the shock. I not only know that he's going to die, I expect him to die. I feel more surprise if he lives for quite a long time, than if he dies within six months to a year. Often, but not always, by the time he dies, I am even ready for him to die. I may have developed a close relationship with him and I'll miss him, but as his life winds down, it may be a great struggle for him to continue to live. He may be hanging on for someone else. At the point when death is inevitable, I offer the highest gift I can and pray for a peaceful transition. I don't believe that we die a minute before our time, or a minute after.

If I have offered him kindness and love in whatever time I had with him, then I, too, feel peace. I don't mean to sugarcoat this for you. It may be very difficult. He may have died long before I was ready to let go. We may have made plans to do many projects. I may go home that day and be angry at my unsuspecting husband. Now, how good do I feel about myself?

I realized that it was important to be able to grieve and let go of my sorrow, no matter how well I knew or didn't know the patient. I rarely get to go to the funerals of my patients. And, often, the funeral may not be the place that feels appropriate to my level of grief, as I see his friends and family in shock and distress.

Grieving is personal and happens in its own time, whether it's in a few minutes or a lifetime. Some hospices require that staff attend funerals. Others schedule discussions with the entire staff to review each person who has died. One residential hospice that I knew of placed a single rose on the patient's bed for twenty-four hours after the patient's death so that staff, and often family, could privately or collectively adapt to the loss.

There was no ritual where I worked. However, a chaplain and I saw the need and decided to create one. Our first thought was to provide an altar in the office where names of those who died could be displayed and candles could be burned on the day of their death. Since some staff members did not come into the office every day, this didn't work for everyone.

Instead, the chaplain came up with a ritual that each staff member could use when they were ready. It just took a few minutes and was as individualized as each person cared to make it. Talking about the ritual and providing supplies for it became part of my orientation to new hospice staff members. The following is only a guideline that can be adapted with your own personal beliefs.

Bereavement Ritual

Name the person who has died and give thanks for them.

Remember the time you shared.

What are you thankful for through having known this person?

What did this person teach you?

What will you miss?

Remember that person's family, loved ones, and friends.

If there was something you did not have the chance to say to this person, take the time now.

Give that person over to the creator of the living and the dead, by using an image of that person in your mind, or by physically lifting your arms as if handing something over.

Light a candle, plant a seed, blow bubbles, or use any other symbol that helps you to offer this person to the God of the universe.

Prayer: O great healer and comforter, thank you for bringing special people into our lives . . . especially _____. Comfort all of us who are filled with sadness at this loss. Help us to remember that all who die are finally released from their suffering and live with you in a place of light and love. We now give _____ over to you. Grant us your strength. May we always be inspired by their memory, for even in death our lives continue to be intertwined. Amen.

It was a gray fall afternoon and there was a chilly breeze, when I received the call in my car that one of my patients, Janis, had died. Usually, I don't have bubbles in the car but I had just bought some for the staff. When I stopped at a busy intersection for a red light, I opened the window, took a deep breath, and blew some bubbles toward the sky. As people saw bubbles floating by their car windows, their demeanor changed. They relaxed and smiled and didn't seem to be in such a hurry. For just a moment, without these strangers even knowing, Janis's life and death touched us collectively, and we all took a deep breath and relaxed before moving forward into our own lives.

ABOUT THE AUTHOR

Jillian Brasch is a registered occupational therapist who has been in practice since 1978. She has provided direct care to hospice patients, co-led an art class for AIDS patients, and led bereavement support groups. She has an extensive background in psychiatry, rehabilitation, and biofeedback, and has published professional articles in *Occupational Therapy Forum* and *Elder Care in Occupational Therapy*. She has lectured at state and national conferences on occupational therapy in hospice care. Jillian lives in Santa Fe, New Mexico.